The Complete Guide To Microsystem Management

Steven K. Roberts

Prentice-Hall, Inc.
Englewood Cliffs, N.J. 07632

Library of Congress Cataloging in Publication Data

Roberts, Steven K., 1952-
The complete guide to microsystem management.

Includes index.
1. Electronic digital computers. 2. Microcomputers.
I. Title.
QA76.5.R494 1984 001.64 83-17817
ISBN 0-13-160556-9

Editorial/production supervision and interior design: *Aliza Greenblatt*

Cover design: *George Cornell*

Cover art: *Steven K. Roberts*

Manufacturing buyer: *Gordon Osbourne*

to Debra and Emily

Printed in the United States of America

10 9 8 7 6 5 4 3 2 1

ISBN 0-13-160556-9

PRENTICE-HALL INTERNATIONAL, INC., *London*
PRENTICE-HALL OF AUSTRALIA PTY. LIMITED, *Sydney*
EDITORA PRENTICE-HALL DO BRASIL, LTDA., *Rio de Janeiro*
PRENTICE-HALL CANADA INC., *Toronto*
PRENTICE-HALL OF INDIA PRIVATE LIMITED, *New Delhi*
PRENTICE-HALL OF JAPAN, INC., *Tokyo*
PRENTICE-HALL OF SOUTHEAST ASIA PTE. LTD., *Singapore*
WHITEHALL BOOKS LIMITED, *Wellington, New Zealand*

Contents

Acknowledgments

I would like to express my gratitude to a number of friends and associates who helped make this book a reality—adding, in the process, invaluable comments and suggestions: Jim Azbell, Kacy Branstetter, Nancy Burkhalter, Dave Buck, Jerome Clarke, Gene Conner, Jim Dudick, Joel Embry, Frank Feczko, Sally Hritz, Jency Kelly, Dan Landon, Tom Long, Lori Opre, Bob Phare, Barbara Potts, Walt Spicker, and John Stork.

In addition, I wish to express my appreciation to the companies that went to the trouble to contribute photos, research materials, and background information: Apple Computer, Computerland, Corvus, Cromemco, Design West, DEC, Dranetz, Dysan, Hayes Microcomputer Products, IBM, Inmac, Media Recovery, Monolithic Systems, NEC, Ring King Visibles, Superior Electric, Televideo, 3M, Uarco, Vector Graphic, and Welco Industries.

Preface

It's not quite as easy as they say. Magazine ads show smiling secretaries blissfully inserting diskettes into drives, while worry-free executives beam from across the room. Computer-store owners respond to the tentative queries of potential first-time users with dramatic tales of computerization successes. Every magazine from *Scientific American* to *Pig American* runs articles about the microcomputer revolution, and there are even preschool-level children's books on the subject.

Yup, it's the panacea we've all been waiting for. Business problems, organizational headaches, human inefficiency—they all go away when you put a computer in your office.

Nonsense!

What about the strange new organizational problems introduced by the machine itself? What about the damage to established human relationships resulting from the imposition of "assembly-line" methods? What about the catastrophic loss of your data files from somebody's greasy fingerprint, the theft of your information, the sudden failure of your printer on the morning of payday, a vendor that becomes uncooperative only hours after the sale, and the depressing discovery that you have spent months building an operation around software that is no longer supported? What about training problems? Insurance? Finding a place to safely protect your ever-greater investment in media? Taking the time out of your already overcrowded schedule to learn enough about the strange new machine to make it something more than an interesting diversion ?

These issues are not often addressed, especially where advertising revenues are involved.

A lot of "microsystem" installations fail. They do so because their owners expect too much of them, fictionally cost-justify them to write off a new toy, or overlook the kinds of issues noted above. Systems that fail involve costs well beyond those of the machine itself, and more than once has a business collapsed around an ill-managed computer that was installed to solve all the problems or perhaps keep up with Jones, Inc.

This book is intended to help you avoid that. It is not a rhapsody about the magic of computers, although my long-established love for the little beasts surfaces now and again. It doesn't have much to do with fitting a hardware and software package to your specific business needs, nor does it presume to compare different models that are going to be rather boring old machines by the time you read this anyway.

This book is about glue—the glue that holds it all together. That doesn't change much with the technology, and is not particularly subject to the variations imposed by different applications. It consists of user-vendor relationships, the machine's environment, maintenance, methods of avoiding catastrophic loss, the needs of the people involved, educational matters, software problems, networking, organizational methods, documentation, and even the myriad gadgets and accessories available to make your operation more efficient . . . or at least flashier.

If all that's under control, the rest is more traditionally manageable. This book is intended to help you avoid disaster.

Steven K. Roberts

1

User–Vendor Relations

1.0 INTRODUCTION

Buying your first computer system can be a somewhat unnerving experience. You haven't yet become jaded by years of exposure to a turbulent industry, but you *have* just made (or are about to make) a significant financial investment in a strange machine with mysterious innards.

Even if it's not your first computer system, any new machine presents its share of problems. Old familiar procedures must be discarded in favor of ones that seem arbitrary and confusing, and every click from the disk drives suggests imminent failure. It's not a time for confidence—it's a time for careful perusal of manuals, and perhaps a few phone calls.

Phone calls to whom? Is there someone out there who cares? Or have you become orphaned through the purchase of an unsupported system?

I offer myself as an example. With a master stroke of bad timing, I switched systems about 20% of the way through this book. The old system, my faithful and reliable "compuservant" for over four years, was shipped south to live out its days in sunny Florida. The new machine, a high-performance system pieced together here from some of the most sophisticated components available today, occupies a fraction of the space that was required by trusty old BEHEMOTH, while delivering substantially higher performance.

The conversion from one to the other wasn't *too* bad, considering the profusion of differences between them: I even managed to transfer all important text files via a serial communication link before bidding final farewell to my old shopworn friend.

So far, so good, it might seem. But here's the catch: This new system sports no manufacturer's name on its front panel (it doesn't even sport a front panel), and there was no sympathetic vendor to call for help when my double-density, double-sided, half-height disk drives started giving seek errors, eating media, and making strange scratching noises. Only the manufacturer of the drives could be called upon for help, and though reasonably interested in supporting its product, it bore no system responsibility whatsoever. I even got the distinct impression that company personnel were suspicious of my nonstandard machine.

This scenario is a bit extreme, of course. These days, only a few diehards still insist on piecing together custom systems to address offbeat environmental or performance requirements that render the available standards inappropriate. But there are dozens of system vendors out there that are only a few steps removed from such madness, and they compete in the same marketplace as IBM, Apple, and the other well-supported, "traditional" machines.

This, of course, introduces a potentially uncomfortable trade-off. For reasons of price or performance, it may be desirable to go with a nonstandard system (and I'm hardly one to argue against this option). But the advantages gained through this approach have to be weighed against those lost: There may not be anyone to call for help if the machine suddenly fails in the middle of the business day. As this chapter progresses, we will have occasion to examine these two opposite approaches, as well as a few others that have arisen during the confused adolescence of this turbulent industry.

1.1 BEFORE THE SALE

There are a lot of companies out there competing for your system dollars, with widely varying products and services to offer. In order to meaningfully address the myriad trade-offs present in the question of vendor selection, let's take a moment to identify the five major types of system suppliers.

- **THE MANUFACTURER.** These days, most computer manufacturers will insist that you work through one of their dealers, since they have learned a few lessons from end-user overloading of their customer service departments. But it is quite possible to purchase a computer directly from its maker, and integrate it at your site with a cathode-ray-tube (CRT) terminal and printer obtained similarly.

- **COMPUTER STORE.** Once only places where hobbyists gathered to drink coffee, marvel at the latest kits, and play "Hunt the Wumpus" on makeshift machines, computer stores have matured into perhaps the most visible manifestation of the microsystem industry. Store owners have shed jeans and sandals for three-piece suits, and the large franchise operations have started looking for MBAs, not EEs. In short, the computer store is likely to be a place where you can find someone aligned with the business world.
- **MAIL-ORDER HOUSES.** If you ever want to aggravate a computer store owner, walk in and start talking about buying a system from a mail-order firm. These companies, whose ads can be found in any small-system magazine, usually offer comparable equipment at substantially lower prices than the stores. Service after the sale might be a bit of a problem, of course, but this approach can definitely save money if you have local talent available to get the system running and keep it that way.
- **THE USED MARKET.** Small systems have been around long enough that there is a healthy market in used equipment. Within this category are the companies that specialize in used machines (such as Newman and American Used Computer—both of which have been around since well before microprocessors) as well as the expected classified ads, swap meets, and private deals. The usual cautions apply, but if cost is a primary consideration . . . *caveat emptor!*
- **CUSTOM SYSTEMS.** Here, we have the proverbial can of worms. There are times when the custom route is unavoidable: you have such bizarre requirements that nothing can be found off the shelf to address them. Unusual interfaces to plant processes or the need for extremely high performance might justify a special design, whereupon you should retain a competent custom firm or consultant. Within this category, we must note the distinction between custom hardware and custom software (we'll have more on that subject shortly).

Clearly, this assortment of potential system vendors complicates the process of buying a machine. The only way to resolve the various trade-offs is to determine, before looking at any equipment, just what you want.

This is not as trivial as it sounds. If you wander into a computer store and say, "I need a machine for word processing," you might suddenly find yourself saddled with an inappropriately scaled system foisted on you by an overzealous salesperson who didn't bother to take the time to determine your needs in more detail. The underlying problem is one of communication: as the purchaser, you are attempting to solve a business problem; as the vendor, the salesperson is attempting to address a technical specification.

This effect is especially acute in custom systems, where a very complex relationship exists between buyer and seller. In my custom engineering days, I frequently found myself in the awkward position of having to translate someone's business problem into a set of system performance specifications before even beginning to quote on the project. As if this wasn't bad enough, I would then discover upon nearing completion of a complex creation that the customer's requirements, as dynamic as his business, had changed. This is more than frustrating: it is expensive. A simple request, such as "Hey, can you guys throw in something that'll make it handle vacation schedules?" might require substantial rewrites of the software. (Of course, a nicely structured system should easily accommodate later changes, but that's not the point here.)

The message is: *Know thy requirements*. If your knowledge of the available equipment is sketchy, you must either hire someone who knows the technology, or retain a consultant to assist in system specification and acquisition. Or you can trust the vendor. But if you are not ready to clearly and unambiguously answer the question "What do you need the system for?" then you have some homework to do before spending any money.

1.1.1 The Learning Curve

But there's still a gap. Even with the system's application requirements well defined, the appropriate choice of equipment (and vendor) may yet be a mystery. In essence, an efficient purchase will consist of an optimal mapping of your present and future needs onto the hardware and software products available in the industry. To do this, knowledge of your "business problem" isn't enough: you must familiarize yourself with the world of computers.

This suggestion is not always well received. "Why," one might ask, "should I take the time and trouble to become a computer expert when I can simply hire a consultant or a programmer to get my system going?"

Well . . . there are a lot of reasons. First, the process of hiring competent computer people is not as simple as hiring a competent typist—in the latter case, performance is easily evaluated on the basis of observation. The industry abounds with people at all levels of computer expertise, and unemployed hobbyists conversant in the technology of games are just as likely to advertise for your consulting dollars as are high-powered system engineers who keep current with available resources and design techiques. Are you equipped to tell the difference? You may never need to write your own applications software, but if you know what it consists of (and maybe a little about how to read it), you will be less likely to find yourself in the uncomfortable position of shelling out money for some mysterious service.

There are even, alas, some in the computer business who thrive on the ignorance of their customers. Even in an industry that is generally honest, enough opportunists exist to suggest the need for caution.

The real problem, though, is simply the fact that computers and all their associated phenomena are relatively new. Even if you are young enough to have been exposed to micros in school, the industry changes so quickly that only the most philosophical of textbooks is still current by the time you read it. This, combined with the fact that computers are perhaps the most useful business tools developed since double-entry bookkeeping, leads to a situation ripe for deliberate or unwitting abuse.

How, then, can one go about acquiring knowledge that will make the claims of computer dealers sound like something other than gibberish? It's not as hard as it sounds: Subscribe to some of the leading journals, spend a few Saturdays wandering around the local computer stores, take a night course in programming, read books, and if you really want to do it right, obtain a small computer for your home.

Wait. This sounds suspiciously like proselytizing for the "home computer revolution," but it's not. The applications of a home system and those of a business or professional machine are probably so far removed from one another that it is profane to even mention them in the same breath. Nor do we suggest that there may be any practical similarity between the $175 box that connects to your TV set and the $6000 one that takes care of your property management. Some dealers might tell you otherwise. Ignore them.

The reason we introduce the idea of acquiring a small computer to play with before committing your business to its big brother is simply an extension of what we said before: Knowledge about this business will go a long way toward making your purchase a successful one. There have been cases of the *rebound effect* in this market, where an uninformed customer buys, on a salesperson's recommendation, a "business system," then discovers after months of frustration and lost time that it is an unsupported, hobby-grade machine inappropriate for any application in which consistent performance is required. The justifiably disgruntled customer then rids himself of the contraption, concludes that all microcomputer systems are worthless, and signs a $600 a month contract with a service bureau. This whole fiasco could be avoided through some self-education on the customer's part.

The industry is yet young enough that the old adage, *caveat emptor,* very much applies. But it is hard to beware if you don't know enough about the technology to recognize junk when you see it.

Lest this all sound hopelessly grim, let me hasten to assure you that for the most part, those who populate the burgeoning computer business are conscientious and competent. Similarly, the days of *turkey systems* marketed as *turnkey systems* are apparently over, and even the most uninformed customer can, with reasonable care, find a machine that will do the job. But as we will point out at various points in this book, the power of a computer is directly related to the person who uses it—and that depends, more than anything else, on knowledge about what it can (and cannot) do.

1.1.2 Casting about for a System

Once you have identified your needs and learned something about the computer marketplace, you are in a position to do some serious looking. But before we comment on that problem, it's time for a disclaimer . . . .

As noted a moment ago, this is a fast-moving technology. Were that not the case, we could spend a few dozen pages talking about various types of systems and their applicability to an assortment of tasks. But even magazine reviews are somewhat stale by the time they see print, and I'm certainly hesitant about dating this book with a celebration of what, by the time you read it, will be passé. Not only that, it would be presumptuous for me to pretend enough familiarity with all possible applications that I could address them in any kind of satisfying fashion. That's *your* business.

So once you know your needs, are conversant with the technology, and have narrowed system selection down to one or two major choices, how are you going to go about filling the hole in your newly readied computer room?

Without further circumlocution, let us put forth a recommendation: Find a competent and supportive computer dealer with a respected product line, a good inventory of supplies, in-house service capability, and excellent references (check them). Then, at least until you are a well-established computer user with a clear idea of further needs, deal with him exclusively.

Of course, finding such a supportive outfit may not be quite that easy. Any reasonably large city will contain dozens of vendors at various levels in the computer retailing hierarchy, and narrowing your choice to one who will stay in business and support your operation is critical and nontrivial. You should use all the care that would be indicated in the selection of a physician, attorney, or accountant.

One approach that has merit is the RFP—the request for proposal. You can specify as unambiguously as possible what your system requirements are, and send a mailing to all of the likely sounding vendors in your area. This technique is hardly new in the business world, but is apparently unheard of by a number of small computer dealers. You can quickly weed out the ones that are too lazy to give you a written response, as well as those who are intimidated by anything approaching an informed customer.

The problem with this, however, is that some very robust and solid dealerships will wad up an RFP and pitch it, as is the case at one high-volume national franchise operation I visited. "We have no time for that," the owner explained. "We carry the highest-quality lines, and keep busy enough just moving systems out the door!" This seems like a cocky attitude, but he explained that the majority of such correspondence calls for custom system configurations or specially modified software, and for all such requirements the store refers customers to consulting or engineering firms. "There's just no margin for customizing anymore—and the legal responsibility, especially in the case of medical billing systems, is intolerable. It's fun, but we can't afford to mess with it."

This hands-off approach to anything nonstandard should not be confused with a lack of support. The computer retailing business has matured considerably since the early days of hobbyist-oriented marketing, and any store worth its logo will offer local service—you bring it in, they fix or replace it. At least one brand of system is supported by the national TRW service network, and others offer their own field personnel. We will have more on that subject later.

But it does lead up to perhaps the major argument for dealing with a local retailer: support after the sale. After settling on a set of system requirements, you will probably find that either the specific machine you had in mind or something very close in performance is available through mail-order channels at a considerably reduced price—sometimes within a few dollars of dealer cost. It is tempting. But if you purchase a machine in this fashion, and then seek local assistance when it breaks, you might find yourself quite unwelcome, even at a dealership of the same manufacturer. Support, even of the relatively low-key "question-answering" variety, costs time (money), and that is paid for by the difference between the bargain rate and full list price.

There are occasions, however, when it does make sense to deal with a discount supplier. Simple accessories—printer ribbons, diskettes, and the like—are no problem, and even such system-level components as CRTs and printers can be thought of as functional black boxes if you would be relatively unaffected by the long turnaround time on a service problem. But it begins to get dangerous beyond this level unless you have the capability to configure the system to your needs, provide your own support, and find the answers to questions without calling for help.

The subject of mail-order computer sales is guaranteed to elicit strong comment from store owners. One dealer I spoke with angrily denounced what he called "mail-order discount prostitution," and cited Apple's move to ban such marketing of their products as an example of the industry's attitude. He had even gone to the extreme, together with a surprising number of other retailers, of abandoning sales of the major computer magazines—since they carry ads for the mail-order houses.

But from the end-user standpoint, there are certain advantages to buying by mail (as long as the requirements noted above are met). If you live far from a large city, support after the sale might be a little thin anyway, and the range of available products on any given dealer's shelves is but a fraction of that represented in a random sampling of catalogs from the larger mail-order firms. Adding, say, an extra interface board to your machine might be cheaper and quicker with a simple toll-free telephone call—as long as, once again, you are equipped to install it and make appropriate software modifications.

Another potential source of lower-cost systems is the used equipment market. As with the purchase of any "preowned" equipment, you stand to save a substantial percentage of the original value if you are willing to take an equally substantial risk. IRS regulations provide for a healthy investment tax credit that can prove more advantageous with a used computer than with a new one, and according to some industry reports, as much as 90% of the cost of a new system can be saved.

The risks can be minimized through the use of the same cautions that would apply on a similar purchase of noncomputer equipment. Obtain written proposals from the dealers or firms involved, specifying not only the exact system configuration but all software and accessories included. Check maintenance records if at all possible, make sure that the products are of a recent vintage that can still be supported by the manufacturer or an independent service organization, and request a commitment on installation assistance and an initial warranty period.

One general note of caution applies to any purchase of a system that is not marketed as a complete package (such as a "mix-and-match" of various vendors' products to meet certain functional or aesthetic requirements): Things aren't always compatible.

The risks are few with such devices as CRT terminals, where the term "RS-232" says (usually) all you need to know about the electrical interface with the computer. But board-level products are a different story, especially with the ever-popular S-100 bus. The problem, it seems, is that the industry took a few years to agree on just what, exactly, the S-100 bus consists of.

It all started back in the mid-1970s with the Altair 8800 system, which was based on a *card cage* containing a number of circuit boards with 100-pin connectors. The definition of the electrical signal appearing on each pin was published, and this made possible the creation of "support products" by manufacturers other than Altair.

But the industry was in its infancy, and each designer who was faced with the task of creating a new S-100 card saw ways to improve the bus and take advantage of some of the unused pins.

The result was chaos. Different vendors sold circuit boards that were ostensibly compatible with one another, but whose electrical characteristics were different to the point of malfunction. It took nearly half a decade for the industry to agree on a standard specification intended to end this mess, but by that time, hundreds of thousands of "S-100" boards were floating around the market.

What this all means to today's computer user is moot—if you buy a standard system off the shelf, the saga of the S-100 is of little concern. But as soon as you unscrew the cover and start adding boards purchased from mail-order firms, used equipment shops, and individuals, you're on your own. I'm not saying it's a mistake (I do it routinely)—only that it is not always as simple as the product advertising would suggest.

All this talk about unscrewing covers and plugging in extra circuit boards raises another set of issues that we should consider before pressing ahead with the business of buying a computer.

1.1.3 Custom Systems

It is not uncommon for a set of system requirements to be unusual enough that no standard package can be found to do the job. This may call for something as complex as a complete system created from scratch, or as simple as a nonstandard bit of programming to support an "off-brand" printer. But no matter what level of custom work is necessary, the fact that someone has to plug in a soldering iron or modify some software introduces a number of interesting problems.

Perhaps foremost among these is the relative isolation you are about to experience. With a "normal" system, you can turn to the manufacturer (who is presumably still in existence), published literature, comprehensive (ahem) documentation, and possibly even a users group—but with a custom system, you might have to depend on the "brilliant weirdo in the back room" of the brash young entrepreneurial firm that did the job. This can be distressing, especially if the person has disappeared upon evaporation of his undercapitalized firm.

A user with custom requirements is in an awkward position. Left with few choices due to inflexible system requirements, he is at the mercy of whomever he can find to do the job. People in the custom business range in competence from one extreme to the other, with everybody from zealous hobbyists to seasoned professionals out there quoting jobs.

Having served time in a custom capacity for a few years before withdrawing in dismay from a brutal marketplace to hang out a shingle as a writer and consultant, I can readily attest to the difficulty of this relationship from the designer's standpoint as well. Perhaps an outline of some of the problems will shed light on the issues that should be considered by the person on the buyer's end of the deal.

- **PROBLEM VERSUS SPECIFICATION.** Here's one that we have already discussed in a somewhat different context: knowing the difference between a business problem and a system specification. All too often, someone will approach a custom shop with a quite reasonable request such as: "We're spending too much money on manual tracking of our guard activity around the plant. Can you build a machine that will randomly issue tours and then monitor their progress through various checkpoints? We'll need printed reports for insurance purposes."

  This is a business problem, and expresses the customer's point of view perfectly. He doesn't care how many bytes of memory are required, and shouldn't have to—he wants a patrol tour system. But after the custom firm evaluates the problem and returns a proposal which, upon acceptance, becomes a system specification, a different situation exists. The designer is now working with an unambiguous task description, and any casual requests for changes to fit ongoing variations in reality mean trouble. Enough flexibility should be specified at the beginning of the relationship to accommodate all but the most bizarre modifications.
- **COST.** A lot of people don't understand that custom work is expensive. Even a little "printer-driver" program requires some harried engineer to sit down with a set of manuals (if he's lucky) and try to figure out how to make something created by one stranger talk to something created by a different stranger. Customers are often staggered by the magnitude of quotations for what, functionally, may be trivial modifications to a standard program or inauspicious little black boxes with a cable out the back and a light on top. "You want $3400 for *that?*"

  The other part of the money problem is connected to the unfortunate fact that most custom work involves some up-front expenses on the part of the system designer. A cash advance may be requested to cover hardware cost or human time.

- **DOCUMENTATION.** This is, no matter how you view it, an expensive part of a project. Any purchaser of a custom system (or even a custom piece of wire) is entitled to a clear and accurate written description of its operation, specifications, theory, and service. Many custom firms, heavily saddled with too much work and too few people, try to pass off a few photocopies of engineering notes—"Don't worry, all the information's right here in this binary dump"—but don't let 'em get away with it.
- **SUPPORT.** I cannot emphasize enough the need for dependable, long-term support on anything that you buy. Unless you are fortunate enough to have in-house system wizards armed with test equipment, spare parts, and exhaustive documentation, you are taking a business risk that should be considered unacceptable. Would you buy a one-of-a-kind photocopier, knowing that there would be no way to get it repaired if it ever broke? Even if it was half the price of a standard machine?

  Of course, from the custom firm's point of view, this is a major pain, often spoken about with snide references to "babysitting," "hand-holding," and so on. But that's not your problem. We'll offer a few suggestions shortly that will give you some protection in case the vendor disappears.

These custom-system considerations all add up to a relationship that is substantially more complex than that which normally exists between a system user and computer store that cashes his check. Questions must be raised concerning the machine's compatibility with equipment that might need to be added later, who will take care of it if the vendor goes out of business, and what constitutes "system acceptance." With some of these questions in mind, which are really just larger versions of those that need to be asked anyway, let's look into the purchase of your system.

1.2 MAKING THE PURCHASE

Once you have reached the point at which you have reasonable confidence in your understanding of the field, the nature of your requirements, and perhaps even a vendor, it is time to take a serious look at making the purchase. We have already outlined a number of the selection trade-offs, and vigorously disclaimed a few others that are functions of either the technology or your business. Now let's work on picking a system and getting it in-house.

It's worth noting that although this book basically avoids the question of system selection (the vast diversity of applications out there rendering such an attempt somewhat absurd), we cannot really ignore it entirely. The majority of you have probably already acquired a machine and are either grumbling about "getting on with it" or riffling, at this very moment, through the succeeding pages to Chapter 2.

But wait! Before leaving us behind, consider: The success of a system installation is dependent not only on the user's sophistication (and that of the system itself), but also on the quality of the support available. This, as we pointed out in Section 1.1 and its subsidiaries, is largely a function of the vendor. So how can the user–vendor relationship be optimized? Read on.

1.2.1 System Selection: The Final Stages

It is reasonable to assume that whatever your application, you possess a solid rationale for your purchase (or lease, or whatever). Some installations, like my own, are rather difficult to quantify in terms of their payoff—I can swear up and down that it saves time and money, but there's no way I could tell you how much.

Most installations, however, are the result of relatively hard-nosed and steely eyed business planning, and here's one of the areas in which something other than intuition and guesswork can be applied to the system selection process.

Determine, first, just what the anticipated savings will be upon obtaining a computer appropriately suited to your operation. This number, perhaps expressed as a yearly figure, should include such things as human time and error reduction, as well as application-dependent figures such as more timely rent increases in a property management business.

Given some idea of the savings expected over your present mode of operation, you can then target a return on investment (ROI) and determine the amount that you can afford to pay each year for a machine. Depending on who you listen to, recommended figures seem to vary from 40 to 75% of the first figure. This allowable cost must include not only the amortization or lease expense of the system itself, but the costs of media and supplies, software updates, consulting, and the *additional* human time (at future wages) that isn't quite obvious upon reading the advertisements. You should also consider the system's salvage value at replacement time.

Armed with these numbers, which can be modified somewhat to incorporate intangible assets and liabilities (such as the public relations value of "computerization" or, just across the balance sheet, the inevitably difficult learning curve that begins even before power is first applied), you can go shopping. Presumably, your earlier research has yielded a number of clues concerning system choices on the basis of available software and general reputation; now you can begin weighing the various options on the basis of their cost-effectiveness.

There's still a healthy measure of "black magic" in this process, since the microcomputer business is characterized by as much diversity in cost/performance ratios as, say, real estate. In fact, it makes sense to round off the three least significant digits in your calculations and just think in terms of thousands.

Anyway, the combination of price (as determined above) and the myriad measures of performance (with the emphasis on hardware and software support) should reduce the number of choices to a manageable minimum. With an eye toward reducing that number to one, let's discuss some considerations that must be juggled with one another during the final stage of system selection.

- **YOUR "COMPUTER PEOPLE."** If you are not the person who is going to be using the machine on a daily basis, you should involve the person who *has* that distinction in the system selection process. As we will be discussing in Section 7.2, computers seem unfriendly enough already. Thrusting your assistant in front of a mysterious machine and handing him or her a stack of barely intelligible manuals is not a very kind thing to do, and will probably ensure some substantial attitude problems.

  Your "computer people" are critically important to your business. Even without official system responsibility, those who spend the most time with your machine will be the ones who know it best—the ones you'll call upon for help and advice when changes are necessary or problems are suspected. It is highly worthwhile to begin those human–machine relationships in a gentle fashion.

  It is not necessary to extend this idea to the level of technical involvement—only to philosophical and aesthetic matters. This would not be the case, obviously, if your application is of an engineering nature (or if you have technical people on tap for any reason), but in a straight business environment it is enough to allow your assistants to check the "feel" of various CRT terminals and perhaps have a go at two or three otherwise-equivalent software packages. Such consideration will not only make them feel like part of the operation, but will give them a much more personal interest in achieving "success" with the system.

- **PERIPHERALS.** Closely allied with this is the matter of peripheral selection. To a large extent, of course, the choices of terminal and printer are determined by the nature of the application: a word-processing environment will (at least until the rest of the world gets used to matrix print) call for a "correspondence-quality" printer, and installations characterized by the need for frequent thick listings will do better to incorporate the fastest machine available within your price range. Considerations of cost and quality enter into the decision as well, together with support of any special features called for by the applications software that is to be used. Modern text-editing programs, for example, almost without exception require a CRT terminal capable of cursor positioning and numerous other special functions.

  Beyond functionality, however, much of the peripheral selection process is arbitrary. In some cases, you won't have much choice—the overall system configuration comes as a "package" that you modify at your own risk. But you will often find a wide array of available peripheral devices. I might suggest a quick look through Section 5.1 if you are on the verge of buying.

- **FLEXIBILITY.** It's obvious that "flexibility" and "expandability" are of primary importance in your purchase of a system—otherwise, you wouldn't be purchasing a system. If you were completely certain that you were never, ever going to do anything but process words, you might go out and buy one of those dedicated machines that does nothing else. It's about the same price.

  That option aside, however, how can you ascertain at this stage the amount of flexibility that you will be able to expect from a given machine? In theory, of course, any computer is as flexible as any other—they all operate on exactly the same principle of executing stored programs in order to shuffle data among their various resources.

  The reality, however, is that a system's flexibility is a function of its maker, the bus structure employed, the breed of the microprocessor chip buried within it, the number of similar systems in use, the age of the design, the type of operating system used, the financial solvency of all involved, and the enthusiasm of its user. Most of these are quite out of your control once you have made the purchase, so it is an excellent idea, if you anticipate much in the way of upgrades, to investigate the implications of some of the technical features that are in vogue at the present time. A bit of investigation will reveal which systems are orphans, which ones are supported only by their manufacturers, and which ones have almost become industries unto themselves. The armload of diskettes you take home now may be awesome, but in a year or so, you're going to read a press release about some incredible new software product—and you don't want to sigh wistfully and wish that someone out there was writing code for *your* machine.

- **REPUTATION.** Many of the advertising dollars shelled out these days are not aimed so much at impulse buying as at the establishment of a familiar name. This is as true in the microsystem industry as it is in any other, and the images thus generated are more or less representative of their associated firms' solidity: all that advertising money has to come from somewhere.

  (This isn't always trustworthy, however, as was the case a few years ago with a very famous West Coast company whose flashy ads occupied prime space in every significant computer magazine. They should have spent some of that money on engineering.)

  This represents another area in which a bit of "nosing around" can pay off. Yes, the *Super-Zoomer 16* is mighty impressive there in the store, backed up by that sexy poster and boasting the fastest multiuser operating system yet—but does it work? Find some customers who have purchased one (if the dealer won't name any, beware), and befriend them. Most people, once burned, will do their best to even the score by warning potential customers away.

  Another issue best noted in the reputation context is documentation. The manuals may look excellent at first glance, but only someone who has waded through them to determine the meaning of an obscure error message and to discover how to recover the file that was just destroyed can give you a realistic idea of how good the documentation is. Don't be seduced by glossy paper and padded binders.

- **UNTESTED PRODUCTS.** How new is the machine you are considering, anyway? If a surreptitious peek at the back panel reveals a very low serial number with lots of leading zeros, considerable caution is in order. This applies at the device, system, and software levels.

  Such concerns should have been on my mind when I committed time and money to the new disk drives whose dramatic malfunction I bemoaned at the beginning of this chapter. By enthusiastically adopting a new product, I have in effect become an unpaid test engineer for the manufacturer, finding and reporting problems. (If anybody ever recommends that you acquire a "burnishing disk" of 1-micron sandpaper to stop your drives from carving grooves in your media, don't trust him or her.)

By purchasing a brand-new design over a less spectacular one that has been around for awhile, you are opening yourself to similar problems. Operating systems and the like are complex, and only now are people even beginning to hit upon programming techniques that allow a reasonable attempt at testing all possible combinations of input data. An industry-standard operating system like CP/M can be counted upon to be well supported and thoroughly tested, even if it lacks the sophisticated features of the latest creations. A measure of conservatism is called for unless you enjoy tinkering and don't *really* need the system working all the time.

- **SUPPORT.** What will you be able to expect in terms of service and applications assistance? This clearly calls for a system backed by a solid manufacturer, but equally important is the dealer and his local resources. If something breaks, Murphy has decreed that it will be at the worst possible time—and do you really want to be told that the machine has to be shipped across the country for repair? Or that "there's this guy who works on 'em in his basement . . . ?"

  You should expect a robust dealership, if that's who you have decided to work with, to offer in-house machine service (or at least a "loaner" while yours is riding around the country in UPS trucks), disk drive alignment, a spares inventory, and at least one competent technician who knows the products you are purchasing. Beware of dealers who offer you a bargain price on the machine, then refer you to a store across town for repair. (Beware also of dealers who tack on a 5% "burn-in and test" charge, then deliver the system in factory-sealed boxes. This has happened.) Anyway, some machines can be supported by field service organizations, which for a substantial monthly fee will take care of both preventive and corrective maintenance. If this expense is justifiable, so much the better.

  It can be assumed that somewhere along the way you will encounter difficulties with the software. It may work perfectly, but I have yet to see a completely self-explanatory system and, as noted earlier, documentation isn't always of the highest caliber. When problems occur, either along your own learning curve or upon discovery of a "true glitch," it is highly desirable to have someone to call. This is explored further in Section 1.3.

- **AESTHETIC APPEAL.** This is a surprisingly important factor in a system's success. You want the machine to be well liked by those who use it—and impressive to those on the "grand tour." A cheaply made cabinet and fuzzy terminal screen not only become galling after a while, but they also indicate less obvious and more insidious shoddiness.

- **COMPATIBILITY.** If any of your close associates, subsidiaries, parent corporations, publishers, customers, vendors, or whatever are committed to a certain type of system in a way that might affect your own activities, by all means take that into consideration. Media-level compatibility with someone close can give you a warm feeling on cold nights.
- **ODDBALL REQUIREMENTS.** Is the system subject to any unusual installation requirements? My "journalistic nomadics" called for a full-function word processor that could live comfortably for a while in a motor home, and this was a major factor in the selection of every component. Other special enviromental constraints might include unusually high temperatures, vibration, noise, dirt, and virtually any industrial setting. There comes a point in the spectrum of environmental abuse whereon even the most rugged of office-grade systems are doomed to an early failure.
- **LAST BUT NOT LEAST.** There's one more consideration that must be given comparable weight to that of everything else we have discussed in this section: *Do you like it?*

1.2.2 What Are You *Really* Buying?

Once you have finally waded through all the options, considered the trade-offs, and quivering with trepidation, pulled out your checkbook, you enter a strange period of relative uncertainty and confusion. Computers are counterintuitive to most people, and that expensive package being loaded into the back of your company car is just a complex amalgam of plastic, glass-epoxy, silicon, gold, carbon, mica, aluminum, and a host of other substances— until you successfully put it to use.

It is the aim of this book to increase the likelihood of your doing just that, but there are a few prerequisite items that must accompany the machine out the vendor's door. It would be wise for us to consider them before going any further.

- **CABLES AND ACCESSORIES.** With the exception of systems sold as a fully integrated package, there is probably a need for a few miscellaneous items before computation is possible. These are excellent bargaining points with the dealer, incidentally, for they can quickly add up to 10% or more of the overall system cost.

Items in this category to keep in mind are CRT and printer cables, diskettes, ribbons, spare printwheels, dust covers, a diskette storage box, and additional software utilities, such as operating system enhancements that may be in the public domain. If the system is being bought on a bid or contract basis, it is worthwhile to specify the list of items down to this level of detail, or you might find yourself stuck with a $200 to $300 invoice for "extras." (See Chapter 9 for a discussion of system accessories.)

- **DOCUMENTATION.** It should go without saying that no system can be considered complete without the appropriate repertoire of manuals covering the hardware, peripherals, operating system, applications software packages, and general operation.
- **WARRANTY.** We'll have more to say about this in Chapter 3, which focuses on maintenance. In the meantime, *be certain* that you have, in writing, a statement of the warranty affecting all parts of your system. If there is an "implied warranty," have it written out in unambiguous terms. It is easy to overlook such things during the thrill of system acquisition, but they can come back to haunt you when something dies after a few hours of use.
- **SERVICE CONTRACT.** You sometimes have two options on out-of-warranty service work. You can pay somebody by the hour to show up and spend an unknown amount of time locating and (hopefully) repairing a problem, or you can pay a flat monthly fee (usually a function of the initial cost of the covered equipment) and receive all the service ever needed at no additional charge. In addition, some service contracts provide for periodic preventive maintenance, which in some cases—especially machines with moving parts such as printers and disk drives—can forestall the need for maintenance of the "crisis" variety.

  The decision to be made, if this option exists, centers around a trade-off: the likelihood of the machine breaking versus contract cost. If your research indicates that the terminal you have purchased has a reputation for frequent failure, it might be wise to pay the $25 per month charges and forget about $600 surprises. But $25 per month is $300 per year, and if the machine dies only once every two years, you can eliminate the nuisance of writing 23 of those 24 checks by skipping the contract. (See Chapter 3 for a more detailed discussion of this.)
- **UPDATE SERVICE.** Normally, upon registration of your software, you are offered the opportunity to subscribe to an update service, which, for a nominal copying fee, keeps your installation current with

the times. It's not a bad idea, because some of the changes are not enhancements, but fixes.

- **INSTALLATION ASSISTANCE.** If this is your first involvement with computers of any form, you are justifiably nervous about the whole affair. I probably won't be helping much with Chapter 2's chilling account of the myriad evils that befall computers and the paranoia that surrounds the handling of diskettes.

  For this reason, it may not be a bad idea to enlist the aid of the vendor in the startup of your system. For him, the basic procedures of cabling the units together, inserting the system disk, booting, and loading the applications software are quite routine, and if you have an hour or so of his time for "handholding," you might be off to a quicker start. In all fairness to the vendors (who will generally insist that they are far too busy for such indulgences), I must point out that the manuals accompanying most modern integrated systems are written well enough for the beginner that this help *should* be unnecessary.
- **SALES DOCUMENTS AND SERIAL NUMBERS.** Here's something else we hope you'll never need: the bill of sale and a list of serial numbers for *all* parts of the system, including the software. It is an excellent idea to keep these physically separate from the machine, perhaps in the same safe-deposit box with your sacred master disks (which we will discuss further in Chapters 4 and 8). Make sure, incidentally, that the serial numbers recorded on the bill of sale match those on the machine. There's potential for abuse there.

1.2.3 The Legal Relationship

Whereas you are the purchaser or lessee of a computer system and have taken into account the foregoing recommendations concerning the accoutrements to said system, you are entitled certain legal rights including, but not limited to, the following: a working machine, freedom to make use of the software but not copy it for others, and a measure of protection from nonperformance on the part of the vendor if your purchase is contractual.

The part about the working machine should be spelled out in your warranty papers.

The part about the use of the software should be spelled out in your licensing agreement.

The part about nonperformance is a complex issue, and will seldom be encountered in an over-the-counter purchase. But let's consider some of the possibilities in a more difficult situation.

A recently publicized case involved a number of medical clinics in a large city, each of which purchased a system from a local firm specializing in medical accounting packages. At about $35,000 each, the systems were built around recognized microcomputer hardware and extensive software written by the firm itself.

It was actually a rather clever package that was impressive from a sales standpoint, although it did contain a number of serious bugs that the firm promised to fix. They made a sincere attempt to do just that, but somewhere in the midst of that process, business faltered and they went bankrupt.

This is not a particularly uncommon event in the computer world, burgeoning as it is with entrepreneurial fervor, but in this case it had more than the usual unpleasant consequences. The dozen or so customers who owned the systems were left with dangerously "buggy" software and unmaintained hardware. The latter problem they solved with little trouble: a local service firm familiar with the machines was willing to provide maintenance contracts. But the software problem was another matter.

They finally located a consulting firm that was familiar with the computer and experienced in that particular dialect of compiling BASIC. Happy with the opportunity to do the work, the consultant showed up at one of the sites, received a demonstration of the problems, and asked for the source code—the original "human-readable" software that had been compiled to yield the working version.

No good. The customers had not received the source, and were thus orphaned: without something palatable to a human programmer, the program might just as well have been a huge sequence of random numbers.

But the story doesn't end here. One of the original owners of the defunct medical billing system firm happened by shortly thereafter, announcing his availability at a monthly rate for "software service"—fixing the original bugs. Or, he mentioned, he would sell the source code for $10,000.

Some customers went for it; others decided to cap their losses by selling the machines and trying again. By buying the systems without any protection against such contingencies, they left themselves open for such unethical abuse.

What could they have done? First, if they had devoted some energy to learning about the computer field, they might have recognized the potential weakness represented by a lack of source code. Although it is very rare to receive the source of *any* piece of business software (I am currently using CP/M and WordStar, and have the source of neither), anything even approaching the level of custom programming is a different matter entirely. Since a large number of business applications involve some measure of custom code, this is not as esoteric as it might seem. If the maker of my word processor were to suffer an untimely (and certainly undeserved) demise, I would have little trouble converting to another brand of system and getting on with my business. But if a medical clinic spends months orienting their accounting to an off-brand system designed down the street, the disappearance of their vendor can be tragic. To whom can they turn?

One good approach was tried: to a consulting firm. But without the source code they were stymied. Recommendation: If you are about to become dependent on a similar small vendor, insist that they place a current copy of the source in escrow as insurance against such an event.

That is not an unreasonable request. They would certainly, and justifiably, be hesitant about simply handing it over (this could lead to all sorts of random and confusing customer-generated variations in their valuable design—not to mention piracy), but the idea of placing it in a safe-deposit box under escrow should not be too threatening.

A further point that should be made in the context of the foregoing fiasco is the level of computer awareness possessed by the customers. The computer industry has, alas, still not reached the level of maturity that would imply a totally error-free, self-adjusting, intelligent system, and as we shall continue to note at various points in this book, the more a user knows about his installation, the better off he is. Although the unfortunate position in which the clinics found themselves can be blamed almost entirely on an unscrupulous vendor, it is probably safe to observe that some additional computer sophistication on their part would have cautioned them up front that potential difficulties existed—or at least softened the impact of the attempted extortion later.

The question of nonperformance becomes even more poignant in the case of a one-of-a-kind custom system. In this case you find yourself paying front money to a firm in expectation of a system that meets an agreed-upon set of specifications. Although snags of various sorts should be expected, most such relationships are ultimately successful—but as in many related ventures, the potential exists for the opposite outcome. All I can really say here, given the wide variety of possibilities that exists, is that your relationship with the custom house should be very well spelled out in a document specifying the equipment to be supplied, the precise function of the program, the on-site training provided, the nature and cost of maintenance, and the steps to be taken in the event of default. It might also be wise, depending on the nature of the installation, to stipulate the extent of "system responsibility" to be borne by the custom firm, especially if their product will be interconnected with equipment and facilities already in existence on-site.

1.3 AFTER THE SALE: ARE YOU ALONE?

No! If you are, then you're doing something wrong. The only users who are alone in this business are diehards like myself who insist, for whatever arcane reason, on a nonstandard custom installation. And even we of the experimental world can eventually find a sympathetic ear if we holler loudly enough when something begins acting bizarre.

I have already mentioned some of the ways in which you are supported after the sale: software update services, maintenance, "handholding," and so on. Let's review those, and look at some others. The industry is intensely active, and you should never find yourself sitting alone and wishing that there were someone else out there who is familiar with the *Super-Zoomer 16*.

- **VENDOR SUPPORT.** Any computer-store owner attuned to the realities of the business world will recognize that there is something to be gained from continued support of past customers. He may moan and complain about being too busy, but he can't afford to alienate you: you may want to upgrade to a more expensive system someday or just pick up a few accessories now and again. So don't be too embarrassed about calling to ask questions.

  In some cases, you might find a stated policy something like this: "Two hours of assistance come free with the system; after that it's $35 per hour."
- **THE MANUFACTURER.** Establishing a good relationship with a few key people at the system's manufacturer is an excellent investment of time and energy. At times when the local dealer can't help, you can probably find, in some back room at the factory, the guy who wrote the code or designed the board.

  The difficult part is getting past the customer service department, which is basically equipped to answer the common questions, issue return authorization numbers, provide the address of your closest dealer, or "make a few notes and get back to you with an answer." This may be all that's needed, but cultivating a key friendship or two through trade-show attendance or sheer perseverance can occasionally pay off—

not only in quicker replies to technical questions but also in the latest inside news about forthcoming products.

Some manufacturers provide additional services that are worth investigating. These include subscriptions to newsletters about their products, software update services, and notification of engineering changes (sometimes called ECOs or "field mods"). This last point can be very profitable—more than once has a mysterious bug been cleared up by an unexpected form letter from the factory advising a little software patch or the installation of a jumper wire from one integrated-circuit pin to another.

- **USER GROUPS.** In any relatively new field characterized by matters of significant complexity, common interests tend to develop. In this industry, they develop along the obvious lines: owners of "XYZ" machines, users of the "PRO-FORMA" software package, physicians with under-$10,000 accounting systems, retired COBOL programmers owning two or more refurbished IMSAI systems and living within three miles of the Monongahela River—all these and more are likely to form societies and publish newsletters. In many cases, notices of their existence appear in journals such as *Byte* and *Interface Age*.

  The amount of value to be gained from such organizations is entirely a function of the people involved, and can range from one extreme to the other. It is definitely worth investigating, if you would find your confidence and knowledge reinforced by others with similar facilities. Even local computer clubs, which are normally oriented to hobbyists, can offer an excellent reservoir of friends, experts, and free software.
- **MAGAZINES.** Of significant interest are the computer-related magazines. In an often-bewildering field, the journals that come and go with the vicissitudes of the industry offer an endless source of tutorial articles, ideas, tricks, and advertisements. With the increasing diversification of what could once actually be referred to as *the* computer field, journals in a variety of subjects can be found to reinforce and aid your efforts. They also represent a hungry market for articles about virtually any aspect of computing, and that may provide an opportunity to become a mini-celebrity for some particularly clever modification that you devised to make your *Super-Zoomer 16* behave like a *17*.

The best "support after the sale," however, is your own knowledge. Before we delve into three chapters on things that can go wrong, it is worthwhile to spend a moment on encouragement.

Once you get past the initial learning curve, during which such procedures as booting the system become almost reflexive, you will develop a rapidly growing understanding of what is going on in there. It's a rather pleasant feeling—certainly in contrast to the confusion that a new system owner experiences during the first two or three weeks.

The ultimate objective of your acquisition, presumably, is somehow involved with an increase in the efficiency of your business. At the basic level, this can be accomplished by acquiring an appropriate software package, running it and entering the required data, but in a truly successful installation, much more is happening.

The key is understanding. I have seen small businessmen and even practicing engineers who, despite the fact that they were using computers on a daily basis, were actually afraid of the machines and unwilling to experiment in any way at all. This renders improbable the style of system use characterized by a growing awareness of possibilities and subsequent implementation of ever-greater increases in efficiency.

Much of the beauty of computers lies in their generality. While they suffer somewhat from a style of information-handling that is fundamentally alien to human beings, they are nevertheless capable of endless variations on endless themes. A box that briskly processes text at one moment can compile a constellation-tracking program a few minutes later and then spend the afternoon printing payroll checks. A robust enough system can do all that at once. But moving beyond the original configuration—recognizing in your available computer time the untapped potential to solve even more problems—is the essence of a healthy and growing microsystem environment.

The key, again, is learning. Although (fortunately), the industry has finally matured to the point whereon one does not have to know anything about the innards of a computer or the operation of its program in order to effectively put it to use, such understanding can only aid in the appreciation of the subtle beauty of computing—an appreciation that will pay off time and time again.

Now, appropriately inspired, past all those awkward questions of system selection and acquisition, let's move on to the task of keeping things running smoothly.

2

The System Environment

2.0 INTRODUCTION

Oddly enough, one of the most universally overlooked aspects of microsystem management is at once the most blatantly obvious: protecting the sizable investment in hardware from environmental abuse. In researching this book, I saw systems in hot corners, their ventilation holes covered by stacks of paper. I saw machines plugged into such flaky power lines that the data displayed on the CRT would shrink and flicker when a nearby air-conditioner compressor started. I saw processors clogged with dust, disks strewn across tabletops, static problems bad enough to require a "Please Remove Shoes" sign in the computer room, and humidity so high that exposed steel fasteners were heavily rusted. That's no way to treat a computer.

Micros are relatively forgiving—at least in comparison to the big systems traditionally associated with the data-processing world—and they are generally safe in an environment that is comfortable for people. But they are often treated with no more respect than desk calculators, and the results of the unwitting abuse are far-reaching. We continue our excursion into the subject of microsystem management with a look at the environmental considerations that are essential to a smooth-running installation. Well before acquiring a system, it is desirable to prepare a benign site.

2.1 POWER AND GROUNDING

Every system that you are likely to encounter has one thing in common with every other: the need for power.

Something has to provide the "oomph" needed to shuffle electrons around in digitally significant ways, and that something is most commonly the ac line, appropriately conditioned by a "power supply" within the system. This is all seemingly straightforward, with little required of the user save the insertion of a plug into the wall.

The potential problems, however, are many. In some installations, the power line to which the computer is connected also serves heavy equipment, and the voltage variations resulting from the cycling of this equipment can confuse the much more sensitive system—possibly in the midst of a critical operation such as a master-file update. Worse, certain types of equipment on the same line can cause voltage "spikes," short transients of sometimes 1000 volts or more, which can actually cause physical damage to the computer. Although very rare, these can obviously be crippling.

In addition, the quality of the power varies, even on a dedicated circuit. This is not necessarily the fault of the utility company: during a recent book project, my system abruptly shut down for a second or so without warning, coming back up with a dead terminal. Dismayed, I called the power company (though with little hope of satisfaction) and was told that a squirrel had committed suicide on the power lines about a block from my house. The current surge through the poor animal's body caused a short power interruption, with every motor and transformer in the neighborhood contributing a few microseconds' worth of high-voltage "spike" as its magnetic field collapsed. It was this effect, not the interruption itself, that destroyed a transistor in my terminal and disabled the system for two days. (There are ways to prevent this sort of thing, which we will consider in a moment.)

Noise in digital circuitry is a classic problem, but with a well-designed system it should not have to be your concern. Hopefully, your machine was designed with an awareness of the proper techniques. But that innocent-looking power cord entering the back of the cabinet is a veritable superhighway of noise propagation, and even well-designed and robust systems have trouble coping with some of the trash that can be found in a sloppy electrical environment. A few factors should be kept in mind during the site-preparation phase of system installation:

1. If at all possible, the computer system should be on its own circuit, with its own breaker. This doesn't guarantee freedom from interference, but it helps.

2. The circuit should be checked by an electrician for a good, low-resistance ground, proper line voltage, freedom from interference and "brownout" effects from nearby equipment, and a lack of potentially dangerous electrical leakage.
3. It should go without saying that a three-wire circuit is a must, but some people quite willingly use "cheater plugs" to adapt a grounded plug to an ancient two-wire socket. No good. The ground is there for a reason.
4. It is characteristic of power wires for noise problems to increase with resistance, which is a function of wire size and length. For this reason, it is wise to avoid extension cords unless absolutely necessary—in which case they should be very heavy duty models.
5. Inevitably, you are going to want to plug other things in, such as modems, extra printers, and so on. Plan ahead and avoid future temptation to use "cube taps" by providing either extra outlets or a heavy-duty switched and fused mutilple-outlet box. If possible, a totally separate power circuit should be provided for non-computer-related accessories, such as coffee pots.

2.1.1 Power-Conditioning Equipment

After our foregoing depressing comments about power problems, we'd better offer some encouragement. All is not lost.

Numerous devices have been spawned by the universality of power problems, ranging from inexpensive components called metal-oxide varistors (MOVs) that can be soldered across the power line to absorb voltage spikes, to massive uninterruptible power supplies (UPSs) that can maintain even large system operation for upwards of an hour in the absence of commercial power.

Ordinarily, no special equipment is necessary in a typical office environment. But sometimes, said environment is in the midst of so much noise-generating equipment that despite outward appearances, some special steps must be taken.

One of the simplest approaches is the use of any of a number of commercially available *surge protectors,* devices that are inserted between the system and the power line. Costing anywhere between $20 and $200, these units can absorb the high-voltage transients produced by nearby lightning strikes, oil burner igniters, and so on.

Power problems, as we have noted, do not always involve wild excursions above the specified voltage. *Interruptions* can be just as annoying, especially since some sinister force always seems to make them occur during file transfers and similarly sensitive activities.

The most obvious solution to this problem is to simply provide a power source that is uninterruptible (Figure 2-1). Based on an appropriately scaled storage battery, the UPS stands ready at a millisecond's notice to replace the standard alternating current with its own internally generated power, preventing unpleasant surprises. UPS cost is a direct function of the length of time it can continue to provide a given amount of power, so it may be sufficient to purchase one that allows the system user just enough time to close files and provide an orderly shutdown. In most "micro" applications, this is the most cost-effective solution.

Before we leave this troublesome subject for more entertaining matters, I would like to suggest one very simple device that can be constructed for under $20 by almost anyone who is handy with a soldering iron. This simple circuit, shown in Appendix B, addresses the problems of brief power in-

Figure 2-1 An uninterruptible power supply (UPS), such as this unit from Welco Industries, can guarantee independence from line fluctuations and loss of ac power. UPSs are available in a wide range of current-handling capacities. (Courtesy of Welco Industries, Inc.)

terruptions such as the one caused by the squirrel mentioned in Section 2.1 (or by a typical thunderstorm). It simply turns short interruptions into long ones. Your work in progress will still be lost (only a UPS can solve that problem), but the likelihood of hardware damage will be minimized. Power problems are all-pervasive and frustrating, but with care, they can usually be beaten.

2.2 INTERFERENCE

Electrical problems are not limited to those related to the power line, even though it violates the sanctity of the computer's cabinet with a direct connection to the noisy world and is thus the major culprit.

No, there are many other things that can cause difficulty. One case that kept the heads of field engineers well scratched for a time involved a matrix printer and a business-band walkie-talkie. They shouldn't have affected each other.

But they did. Occasionally, a wandering security guard would pass near the computer room and innocently use his radio, causing a particularly sensitive position-sensing circuit inside the printer to grossly misinterpret reality and pass erroneous information to the control logic. The print head would then fly to the rightmost position on the page, and the wires, still pulsing with data, would eat a little hole in the platen.

This problem was obviously rather hard to fix until somebody noticed, quite by accident, the correlation between the guard's activity and the printer's malaise. In this particular case, the fault lay with the printer design, but it is far more common for such interference problems to be traceable to poor cabling between units.

Two things must be remembered when wiring digital devices (such as computers and their peripherals) together. First, any wire is an antenna and will have a voltage induced in it by nearby electromagnetic fields, which can come from other wires, telephones, CRTs, motors, fluorescent fixtures, static discharge, and, of course, radio transmitters. Second, digital circuitry responds with surpassing efficiency to noise of even a volt or two, making those induced voltages particularly troublesome.

This leads to the suggestion that interconnecting cables should be ensconced in well-protected bundles (which do *not* include power cords!), and routed well away from the noisy devices noted above. They should not be unnecessarily long, especially if they carry *parallel* interface lines rather than the *serial* ones commonly associated with terminals, modems, and the like.

In addition to cable care, system cabinets should be well grounded, and not just for human safety. A good ground system acts as an electromagnetic shield, in the process alleviating some of the dangerous effects from that perennial cold-weather scourge of the information-processing world: static (which we will consider in more detail shortly).

And as if all that isn't bad enough, a problem that will continue to pervade the industry for some time also involves interference—but with the operation of other devices by the computer, rather than the other way around. Of course, some people are data-processing chauvinists, unconcerned with nearby television sets (what's on TV worth protecting during business hours, anyway?) as long as The Machine is working correctly. But this sort of attitude can cause friction among neighbors—or departments, if another part of your company requires radio communications of any type (including FM stereo).

Problems in this area are best solved by a good engineer with a handful of capacitors. Decent cabinet grounding and cable shielding at the system end, and appropriate filtration at the radio end, should markedly reduce the interference effects noted.

2.3 HEAT AND HUMIDITY

Concern over thermal problems is something traditionally associated with large data-processing systems, which are normally coddled in a large room under the care of air-conditioning and humidity control systems. These big computers typically dissipate so much power (in the form of heat) that some means must be used to spirit it away from the machines themselves lest they self-destruct.

This has led to some humorous fiascos over the years. One of the famous war stories involves a new world headquarters for a multinational corporation, built sometime in the early 1970s. The designers, being forward-looking and inventive folk, noticed that the amount of heat generated by the four maximum-configuration IBM systems was significant enough that it could make a major dent in the building's winter heating requirements. Why discard perfectly good heat and then create more with expensive fossil fuels?

The building was therefore designed with a much smaller than normal heating plant, with vast ducting connecting the computer room into the air-handling system. In the summer, the system would be air-conditioned as usual, but in the colder months, it would be cooled, effectively, by *return* air from the rest of the building.

But while construction of this innovative scheme was under way, the data-processing department noticed that one fancy new Amdahl computer could accomplish everything that they had originally planned on doing with the four older machines. So they bought one.

The building was completed, the computer arrived, and everybody moved happily into their new offices and went to work. Then winter rolled around, and everybody froze. It seems the computer wasn't producing its share of the building's heat.

Amid the thunder of rolling heads, a hastily constructed auxiliary furnace was patched onto the side of this otherwise architecturally pleasing building.

Such tales can't help but evoke indulgent smiles in the world of microcomputer users. With machines that can be carried *in toto* from room to room by one person in one trip, the very idea of the fiasco described above is absurd. But it does illustrate a set of thermal realities that are no less compelling in a desktop computer than in a machine with 1000 users. The fact is, the operation of electronic circuitry involves certain losses that manifest themselves in the form of heat which, if allowed to build up within the cabinet, can destroy the very circuitry that produced it.

Commercially available microcomputer systems and peripherals are, theoretically, already well designed for heat dissipation. (Not always: the CRT terminal that I used for a number of years had to have slots cut in its top with a sabre saw to prevent the monthly destruction of circuit boards.) But the problem is encountered most often in the user's environment.

The most frequent transgression is the coverage of ventilation holes with stacks of paper, manuals, or even diskettes. (This last one is doubly dangerous: while thermally stressing the equipment, the magnetic media become warped and distorted.) Equipment cooling depends, whether there is a fan or not, on a free flow of convective air. If this is blocked, dangerous accumulations of heat can develop within minutes.

At system installation time, future temptation to cover every available horizontal surface with papers can be reduced somewhat by providing a spacious area around the terminal and printer, together with plenty of storage space for diskettes, manuals, spare ribbons, and so on. In addition to this, the locations of fan grilles, ventilation slots, and the like should be noted, and given plenty of free space.

It is also wise to consider the thermal effects of the sun's rays (remembering the seasonal variations in azimuth, of course) at system installation time. Solar energy isn't always wonderful.

In some computers of a more industrial nature, it is not uncommon to find foam or expanded aluminum air filters mounted adjacent to the fan.

These are a mixed blessing. They can keep potentially troublesome dust from entering the enclosure, but if they become clogged, they can prevent the cooling of the machine. We'll have occasion to consider this further in Chapter 3, but notation should be made on somebody's calendar to clean the filters periodically.

Closely allied with problems of heat are those of humidity. Too little (below 40 to 50%) is an invitation to the devastating effects of static electricity (Section 2.4), and too much (over approximately 80%) leads to mildew, corrosion, and soggy documentation. In really extreme cases of high humidity (such as business or process control systems located in Venezuelan jungles or the American Southeast), it is even possible for fungal growth to take over the circuit boards, altering their electrical characteristics to the point of malfunction.

In colder climates, humidity levels during the winter months can drop to the point whereon a carpeted space is alive with static, and people who live and work around computers are forced to adopt all sorts of bizarre permutations to their daily activities in deference to their machines' sensitivities. It is not uncommon to see normally staid executives slip off their shoes, discharge to a screw in the light switch, then tiptoe across the room to the computer and, wincing, reach out to touch it. That's ridiculous, but all too often, necessary.

2.4 STATIC ELECTRICITY

Such absurdity reached crisis proportions in an installation that I once had the misfortune of supporting as a field engineer. The system in the computer room was far from the micro level, but scattered about a large office building were dozens of CRT terminals at employee workstations. The static problems were more than just a nuisance: carelessly touching a terminal without going through the discharge ritual not only "glitched" the screen, but transmitted garbage to the host computer, which was far too dumb to deal with it casually (no error-detection logic). Files were thus lost or changed, functions were randomly invoked or aborted, and so on.

The fault was in the design of the terminals. Logic circuitry will quite happily respond to any input transition of a couple of volts, caring little whether it is "reasonable" in the context of its normal data. Considering the fact that static discharge generates pulses of thousands of volts, it's not surprising that problems can occasionally result.

The trick, of course, is keeping the high-voltage trash from making its way into the logic circuitry. But all too often, the designers overlook some small matter like shielding, and the user is stuck with a sensitive machine. Such was the case in that office building, and we harried field engineers spent weeks chasing around with aluminum foil, antistatic spray, grounding mats, low-resistance cables, replacement circuit boards, and finally, whole new terminal cabinets that incorporated a measure of shielding capability. (Shortly after all that work was done, the customer changed computer vendors.)

If you are unfortunate enough to have a static-sensitive system, there are a few things you can do to ease the pain. Keep the humidity levels within range (about 40 to 80%) by adding a humidifier to your building's air-handling system. Add a grounded "antistatic" mat for the operator's chair (Figure 2-2), and verify the quality of all system grounds. Some manufacturers let the metal cabinet of the processor electrically *float*—unconnected to anything—and this can be fixed by simply running a heavy wire from the cabinet to the main ground point (*not* to the "cold" side of the ac line!). In truly extreme cases, the system can be moved to an uncarpeted area, the

Figure 2-2 An antistatic floor mat allows charge to dissipate before it can cause data loss or equipment damage. (Courtesy of 3M.)

existing carpet can be replaced with tile, or special antistatic carpet can be installed.

It is important that everything in the room have a discharge path to ground, to prevent static buildup. A nylon carpet is about the worst approach—human beings and equipment cabinets all "float" relative to each other and such events as the contact of one swivel chair with another will generate enough noise to create problems (believe me—I've lost more than one file that way). Equipment furniture (such as printer stands) should not be insulated from the floor by plastic or rubber casters, and people should be discouraged from wearing nonconductive shoes.

Even if the system itself is well designed for static immunity, processes (such as EPROM programming) that bring sensitive components into contact with the outside world must be done with care. (A simple trick here is the provision of a ground point immediately adjacent to the EPROM socket, allowing the hand bearing the chip to give up its charge through something other than the sensitive device.)

A surprisingly sensitive point of contact with the system is the *reset* line, which normally appears as a front-panel pushbutton. Some systems allow for the convenient placement of a remote reset switch on the end of a cable—something that seems like a pretty good idea. (If the system is out of reach and the reset button is on the back, it's much nicer to have another one available right beside the terminal.) The problem with this is that the circuitry in the computer connected to the reset signal is typically very sensitive to short pulses (like noise), and that long *antenna* wadded up behind your desk and lying across the floor is an invitation to disaster. I once battled a mysterious static problem for months before a process of elimination finally implicated the remote reset switch.

One last static tip: If you find yourself handling circuit boards, it is good to adopt the practice of touching a person before handing him or her a board full of logic. This is not only a good way to make friends, but the static difference of potential between you might otherwise swiftly and silently destroy the board at the moment of contact.

2.5 CONTAMINATION

It is generally well known that industrial environments pose some difficult problems to equipment in the general area of dirt and airborne contaminants. But even the relatively gentle office environment presents some environmental influences in that category that should be considered both before and after system installation.

Fans, as we pointed out earlier, are a mixed blessing. While they cool the enclosure, they speed the introduction of airborne dust and other materials. If, as is the case with many systems, the negative air pressure inside the fan-cooled enclosure causes air to be drawn in through the floppy disk drives, the sensitive magnetic media are constantly being exposed to sticky cigarette smoke deposits, gritty dust, hair, industrial pollutants, and who knows what else. A nice, albeit partial solution is to keep the room clean and forbid smoking.

Some contaminants have more obvious and direct effects. I have heard a few horror stories about microscopic airborne fibers from the many new products that use graphite as a structural material—conductive, of course. I also witnessed a humorous but potentially catastrophic situation in a highly critical control application, based on an old IMSAI 8080 system. The machine became flaky. A kick would send it reeling—another would bring it back to reality. Eventually, a service call brought the system designer himself, armed with the latest in sophisticated diagnostic tools, spare boards, and manuals. Eyeing the machine professionally and responding to the customer's explanation of its behavior with a studied "hmmmm," he executed a few obligatory test routines and then bent down to remove the cover.

Anticipating a bad connection because of the system's apparent sensitivity to vibration, the engineer pulled one of the memory boards for a visual check of the edge connector pins. He drew back in horror as something white and gooey dripped onto his pants. He looked inside the hapless IMSAI and noted that the socket from which the board had been pulled was nearly full of the same substance. So were ten or so others.

It turned out, after much head scratching and silent appeals to various deities, to be a mixture of detergent and floor wax. Over a period of many months, the frequent floor care rituals of the custodial staff had produced quite a bit of airborne material, which was drawn into the system enclosure by the fan and blown across the boards. It collected on the cards, eventually puddling in the edge connectors to produce intermittent behavior and a rather awesome mess. (The sophisticiated diagnostic equipment remained in the corner as the engineer spent the afternoon with a scrub brush. It's not always a glamorous business.)

That, of course, was rather atypical. Much more common is coffee spillage, dust from continuous forms, "house dust," and similar debris. The terminal on which I started writing this book once suffered from a rowdy cat's upending of an inappropriately placed bud vase, dumping water onto the keyboard. (At least it wasn't Coke.) Careful drying with compressed air and a hair dryer restored normal operation.

It is tempting to take these problems lightly, and perhaps the relatively frivolous tone of the floor-wax tale suggests that we relegate such matters to that dubious category called "computer war stories" (Section 3.4). But the overheating of an expensive and much-needed system because of a clogged filter is no laughing matter; nor is the corrosion of a CPU board due to a spilled soft drink or even human perspiration. In some environments, particularly those blessed by petrochemical processes, smelting or even spindrift from a nearby ocean, the air itself can have long-term corrosive properties.

This all boils down to a recommendation. Respect the machine. We all tend to get a bit callous about hardware in daily use, especially after the "new" wears off. But a little extra attention paid to cleanliness will pay off—in longer periods of service between failures and fewer mysterious glitches that can never quite be pinned down. As we shall see in the next section, disks in particular can create incredible difficulty if not protected from the environmental ravages discussed here (and many others as well).

2.6 MEDIA CARE

Much of the hubbub associated with the environmental requirements of small systems can be traced to the sensitivity of diskettes and other magnetic media to a variety of abuses, ranging from ringing telephones to the fingers of the curious or careless (Figure 2-3).

Much of what we say about floppies applies as well to hard disks, but there is a key difference: even though hard disks are, at their heart, far more sensitive to airborne particulates, they are generally much better protected from the environment. Floppies present naked magnetic surfaces upon removal from their envelopes, and they can be written on, bent, overheated, crushed, moistened, and exposed to magnetic fields. Hard disks are typically ensconced within rigid cartridges or, if they are nonremovable, within the mechanically stable and air-filtered confines of the drives themselves. Most of the following is thus aimed at users of diskettes.

Since the diskettes themselves are simply circular pieces (either $5\frac{1}{4}$ or 8 inches in diameter) of Mylar coated with a magnetic oxide material upon which data are recorded, it follows that they are sensitive to magnetic fields. Such fields are generated in an extremely controlled fashion by the head assembly that traverses the rotating media under system control, but they are also produced wantonly by CRT terminals, telephone ringers, speakers, power supplies, and almost any steel tool or office implement (scissors, paper clips, and so on) that has been lying around for a while. This suggests

Figure 2-3 The reliability of diskettes—the data storage medium upon which much of the industry depends—is a function of the care given to their handling. (Courtesy of Dysan Corporation.)

the first requirement for diskette care: keep them away from stray magnetic fields.

This can be rather difficult. I have occasionally walked about my computer room after reorganizing the equipment, carrying a box of 150 or so floppies, looking for a safe place to set it down. It leads to paranoia.

But if magnets were all we had to worry about, things wouldn't be so bad. Another perennial problem—of probably greater severity—is dirt.

Dirt comes in a lot of forms, some of which are not at all obvious. If particles of dust or grit find their way inside the floppy's jacket (that square plastic carrier in which the circular disk itself rotates), they may be carried by media rotation into some obscure corner, there to lie in wait for many months. Most likely, they will be trapped by a soft liner that is designed to continuously clean the surface of the media by trapping such material.

So far, this sounds harmless: the liner is just doing its job. But months later, someone might grab the disk at just the spot where a particularly dangerous particle resides, scratching the magnetic oxide coating at that point. Months after that, some file save operation might write data over that very spot, and *voilà:* the console displays one of those positively chilling DISK ERROR messages. The introduction of dirt into a disk will, if it doesn't cause immediate problems, create future failures whose origins are impossible to determine.

It's easy, of course, to just keep the computer room reasonably clean and settle back, complacent in the belief that diskette contamination is the last of your worries. But does anyone smoke around the machine (Figure 2-4)? Is the system located in an industrial area with dirty air? Have any operators touched the exposed magnetic surface—even once, briefly—with a finger or two, then slipped the disk back into storage with the others? Time bombs, all of them. The oils from fingerprints are particularly infamous, and *will* cause problems.

Other contaminants are also troublemakers. Any liquid will ruin a diskette (or at least cast its integrity into such question that it is psychologically advantageous to just pitch the thing), and the strong vapors of certain

Figure 2-4 Smoking around the computer should be discouraged—for the health of the machine, the media, and the operator.

aromatic hydrocarbons can do strange things to the plastics and bonding materials of which the diskette is made.

Such concerns lead to a few more media-care suggestions (Figure 2-5). Avoid laying unprotected media on the desk (or any other surfaces—they are usually dustier than they look). Instruct all operators in proper handling. Do not allow the disks to be crushed or compressed—it can force trapped particles into the magnetic oxide surface. Try to prevent cigarette smoking around the computer (this handily provides a defensible explanation for a "NO SMOKING" rule). Keep all beverages, foods, pet hairs, insects, house dust, paper dust, and dirt away from the diskettes, and also keep the drives themselves clean. Be careful when operating the system with dirty hands, and close the window when it rains.

And then there's heat. In a computer room that is comfortable for human beings, it is unlikely that diskettes will be exposed in their storage

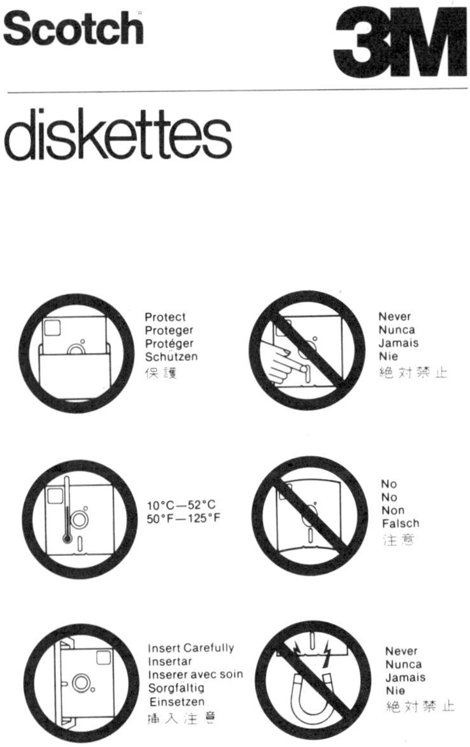

Figure 2-5 Virtually all diskette jackets offer handling suggestions designed to remind the user about the evils of dust, magnetism, heat, fingerprints, bending, and proper insertion. (Courtesy of 3M.)

box, binder, or whatever to temperatures outside their recommended limits (which vary according to manufacturer: 10 to 52°C or 50 to 125°F are typical). But, unfortunately, the disks don't spend all of their time in storage.

I mentioned the most common form of thermal abuse earlier: laying the media on top of a CRT or other cabinet containing active electronic circuitry, not only blocking the vent openings and threatening the hardware, but overheating the disk as well. You can find enough heat on top of some CRT terminals to soften and warp the jacket, virtually ensuring a subsequent *seek error* or other future failure.

Also, transporting the troublesome little things can cause problems—quite obviously in an automobile parked in the sun, but also in such characteristically safe havens as an attaché case or shipping container.

In general, thermal problems can be held to a minimum by simply avoiding the obvious transgressions and allowing the disks time to stabilize when moving them from one place to another. It takes a few hours for the Mylar base to return to its normal dimensions after it has been carried through a blizzard, but there should be no permanent damage.

On the general subject of disk transportation, it should be noted that one's only copy of anything should never be mailed (actually, one shouldn't have an "only copy" of anything). When it is necessary to ship a diskette through the mail, it should be packaged very well as protection from external magnetic fields, dirt, bending, and temperature extremes. A reasonably safe method is the creation of a sandwich with two pieces of corrugated cardboard (their "grains" perpendicular to each other), the insertion of that into a plastic bag, and the subsequent insertion of all that into a padded or bubble-lined shipping envelope. Beware of the old-style padded shipping bags—the shredded paper used for the cushioning is a heavy dust source. This whole problem can be avoided with the use of special diskette shipping containers such as those marketed by Inmac and others (see Appendix A).

Storage of the diskettes is another problem. By this time, you may be thoroughly paranoid about even touching the crazy things (oh yes—be careful when you do to avoid static discharge), and the very thought of a lot of them together holding all of your precious data may be unnerving. It should be.

The idea of having all one's files in the same box is thoroughly frightening, and that condition should be avoided at all costs. We will consider this subject much more thoroughly in Chapter 8, but at this point, let's just note that despite the relative rarity of "hard" failures, they do happen, and diskette storage and handling practices should be adopted that will keep your business going even if a file does get destroyed by a rampant fingertip or a magnetized pair of scissors.

Storage requirements are fairly obvious. The disks should be protected from all of the evils described so far, they should neither sag nor be under compression, and they should be convenient, organized, and clean. The disks, and all things that touch them, should be inspected periodically by someone in a position of responsibility for the information contained thereon.

The last point that needs to be made on the care of diskettes involves the real point of their existence: use in disk drives. They must, first, be inserted properly (failing to do this is a frequent, and potentially expensive, error). Once you've been around the system for a few days, this is totally obvious, but if anybody else is ever going to have occasion to use the machine, it might be wise to stick labels on both the disks and the drives that must be visually matched to ensure proper insertion.

Second, it is not a good idea to slam the drive door once the disk is in, especially on some brands of minis that have an annoying propensity for crinkling the edges of the center hole where the hub is supposed to hold on to the Mylar sheet (you can buy some little white adhesive-backed vinyl rings to prevent this). Be gentle. Similarly, they should be inserted and withdrawn slowly, not with the impatient violence that so often characterizes the coffee-wired and deadline-driven programmer.

Third, it is worthwhile to avoid turning the computer on and off with the disks installed. I have never had problems directly traceable to this source, but some systems are famous for occasionally writing garbage on disks that are resident in the drives during power cycles. I personally think it's a case of poor design (how can you plan for a sudden power failure without a UPS?), but it is, at least at this stage of the industry, an unfortunate fact of life. If you are shutting the machine off or turning it on, have the doors open.

So. If you haven't been frightened away from diskette use by this time, let me hasten to assure you that the worst is over. Let's put all that behind us with a very quick look at the problems of vibration and shock, then we can close out this chapter with a discussion of computer room layout and planning.

2.7 SHOCK, VIBRATION, AND SHIPPING

In the industrial design milieu, a considerable amount of engineering effort goes into making equipment ruggedly capable of withstanding the continuous environmental assault to which it is typically subjected. A CRT terminal designed to last for many years in an office environment might make it a week—if that—in a foundry.

But even nonindustrial systems are routinely forced to contend with a variety of environmental influences that are anything but gentle. Some we have mentioned: power-line spikes and static surges measuring well into the thousands of volts, corrosive liquids (potable though they may be), and airborne contaminants. We can add to that list human perversity, incompetence, sporadic maintenance, and physical abuse. In that last category is included the mechanical shock associated with improper handling, shipping, and so on.

The kinds of problems that can result from physical shock to a machine are many. First, if the shock is of a recurring nature (better called *vibration*), wires can be stressed to the point of developing intermittencies, and chips and circuit boards can work their way right out of their sockets. The net effect of any vibration-induced problem is likely to be general "flakiness," accompanied by sensitivity to kicks and swats on the side of the cabinet.

One very famous problem of this nature resulted from the combination of microscopic vibration over a period of years with an unfortunate characteristic of the wire chosen by the manufacturer for the interconnection of thousands of pins on a giant backplane. The insulation was Teflon, which, although it has excellent thermal characteristics, tends to "cold flow" over time when it is highly stressed—such as around a tight and sharp corner. Hundreds of these systems infuriated their owners, as they would suddenly crash in response to the passage of a truck, requiring a curse and a kick to restart.

In the systems of which we speak, this sort of thing is hopefully rare. Perhaps the worst vibration problem to be faced is in the printer, which too often is located on a flimsy stand rather than a good solid support. As the head flies back and forth, the stand wobbles, possibly banging against another cabinet and, well, there's just a lot of vibration. It not only stresses cables and connectors, but it's bad for the mechanics of the machine.

Some unfortunate CRTs find themselves subjected to that particular breed of computer users who, for some reason, probably involving a primitive reaction to the threat of a nonhuman "intelligence," tend to bang with violent authority on the keyboard. The RETURN key, in particular, seems to receive the bulk of this abuse, since it is usually the key that causes a command line to be executed. It must be remembered that something has to absorb that shock, and it is probably a circuit board full of chips, some of which are in sockets. If the key itself doesn't give out, something else probably will.

Another whole class of vibration and shock problems is presented when we take a machine out of its stable home and move it someplace else—down the hall or across the country. It borders on belaboring the obvious

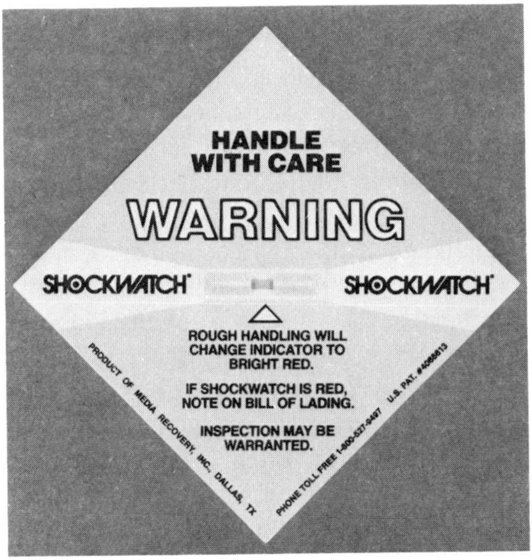

Figure 2-6 Shockwatch label provides unambiguous indication of excessively rough handling of sensitive equipment during shipment. (Courtesy of Media Recovery, Inc.)

to suggest gentleness in handling, but once a disk drive or other peripheral has been boxed and handed over to a carrier, it's out of your control. Aside from extremely careful packaging, the best suggestion is probably to incorporate a small and inexpensive device called *Shockwatch* (Figure 2-6), which will change color if a certain "G" force is exceeded. This won't straighten out the bent platters on your Winchester disk drive or reassemble an imploded cathode-ray tube, but it will strengthen your case against the carrier if a package was severely mishandled.

Good luck, and don't forget to let everything thermally stabilize at the end of its journey. This stabilization period can be well spent in close inspection of all moving parts (and those that moved, but shouldn't have).

2.8 COMPUTER ROOM LAYOUT

Before abandoning the subject of the system's environment, it would be good to take a more general view of it. The overall layout of the computer room can do much to minimize problems such as those noted in this chapter.

The best time to consider such pervasive topics, of course, is prior to system acquisition. If the newly purchased machine has a well-planned home to move into, life will be much easier for it—and for the people who will be spending thousands of hours interacting with it.

Many of the ideas that have to go into a computer room's overall plan are involved with human comfort and efficiency, and these are considered in much greater depth in Chapter 5. Here, let's view the subject primarily from the system's standpoint, with some larger organizational questions thrown in.

A good place to begin in planning a computer room is the determination of furniture layout and work space. If you are starting from scratch, this information can in turn be used to guide the installation of sacred power outlets (as opposed to those of the utility type, available to anyone who needs them). It will also yield insight into proper locations for lighting fixtures, fire extinguishers, and so on. But we're getting ahead of ourselves.

A number of simultaneous, often conflicting requirements must be juggled during the planning of a computer room, even a small one. The process is a little easier if you start with a scaled-down sketch of the empty room on a piece of graph paper and similarly scaled cutouts representing all of the machines and pieces of furniture that need to be installed. There are a number of things to keep in mind during the juggling process.

- **EFFICIENCY.** Typically, the computer system will be used for a variety of tasks, most of which can be broadly characterized by the appropriate processing of some kind of input to produce some kind of output. In the word-processing case, the input may be a rough collection of notes or copy to be edited, and the output is printed text. In the software-development case, the input is probably a listing of the previous revision astrewn with cryptic markings, and the output is a new listing and a new file. And so on. The computer room layout should accommodate these types of activities by providing the physical space for input materials on a work surface beside the CRT (preferably deep enough for an "opened" continuous-form listing—at least 22 inches front to back). Some dedicated word-processing installations provide copyholders beside the screen that float above the desk surface, but make sure there is room as well for books, notes, and other reference materials.

  It's a good idea to include in the "efficiency" category some consideration of work flow—there should be no backtracking, and input and output materials shouldn't have to compete for the same precious few square feet of desk space.
- **HUMAN COMFORT.** It is a real pain to try to operate a system—alternately typing on a CRT terminal, swapping disks, and rolling

about in your swivel chair to consult manuals, rip paper off the printer, and access the trash can—if the physical space available is limited by other pieces of furniture and nearby walls. Just be sure to leave adequate space, provide good lighting, and allow for free movement. Remember that someone is going to spend a lot of hours with the machine—it should be every bit as comfortable as a good office.

- **SYSTEM ACCESS SPACE.** Moving little cutouts around on a piece of graph paper in an attempt to hit on a workable layout is deceptively simple if you don't keep in mind the actual space requirements of some of those machines. A printer, for example, is usually much smaller than the actual space that it requires during use (by a factor of 2 to 3), and other pieces of equipment—such as the computer itself—require additional space for cooling, cabling, access to power and reset switches, and ease of maintenance. One should consider manufacturers' recommendations for such space in the dimensions of the cutouts, with the physical boundaries of the machine drawn in for reference.

  As I mentioned, the printer is quite a space hog. Not only does the paper that it churns out have to have someplace to go, but it must be possible for the operator to get at it. There needs to be space on at least one side of the printer so that calisthenics are unnecessary.
- **FILE AND CABINET SPACE.** If your repertoire of cutouts doesn't include a file cabinet, get out the scissors. As we will discuss in Chapter 8, the presence of a computer system, however small, tends to generate volumes of paper and miscellaneous critical information that must remain readily available. If this is not anticipated at system installation time, this paper can quickly take the form of numerous piles and miscellaneous desk clutter, and it is better to anticipate that with a dedicated file cabinet of at least two drawers.

  Similarly, there will need to be space for diskettes (both blank and otherwise), paper, ribbons, felt pens, scratch paper, software listings, spare boards, cables, and all sorts of other things. It is probably safe to say that no amount of cabinet and file space will later be deemed superfluous.
- **TRAFFIC.** Those thousands of hours with the machine that we mentioned a few moments ago are a lot more pleasant if people are not constantly wandering through the computer room, stopping now and again to chat, smoke, and leave half-empty coffee cups precariously balanced on the edge of the disk drive cabinet. If the building design is such that the computer room is enroute to something else, try to partition the room such that a deliberate effort is required to enter the operating space.

On the other hand, you wouldn't want to restrict human flow so severely that it is impossible to walk around. Excessively narrow passages, a pain to begin with, become a serious problem when maintenance personnel need to drag equipment in or out—or when you try to install the machine in the first place (the doors, I presume, are wide enough?). Access to the computer room from other parts of the building should not be particularly difficult, especially if the system's information load is heavy enough to justify such "big system" accoutrements as carts designed for the transportation of listings and media.

- **SECURITY.** Every installation has different requirements here, and we shall save discussion of file and data protection for Chapter 4. But when designing the computer room, you can help matters somewhat by providing for restricted access to the facility.

  There are a lot of ways to do this, and only the requirements of your business can determine just how serious you need to get about access control. At the lowest level is the simple use of a room with only one door—perhaps with a pushbutton lock; at the highest level is the use of a *man trap,* wherein a person desiring access must pass through a locked anteroom, receiving clearance in the process from a guard or electronic identification device. This is a bit heavy for a microcomputer system, but you never know.

  More typical business systems, although not justifying the investment suggested by the man trap, can nevertheless profit from attention to access control and security at the beginning of system installation. Accounting software, payroll, receivables, work in progress, inventory, custom jobs, books—all sorts of things can be totally dependent on the machine, and some of them may have value to others whose persuasions are not necessarily aligned with your own. Think about it. Should just anyone be able to sit down at the terminal and examine accounting files?

- **NOISE.** Some pieces of equipment, notably printers and hard disk drives, generate considerable noise. In time, this may wear on the nerves of those condemned to spend hours at the console, and it may be wise to locate particularly loud machines behind a partition. In the case of the printer, the partition should be transparent so that the operator can keep an eye on the machine and rush to its aid in the event of a paper jam.

  If the installation is in a building that houses raucous equipment (such as in a printing business), the computer room should have a door (it should anyway in such a place, to keep dust to a minimum). Much of this is purely for the aesthetic benefit of the human beings involved, for you probably have an investment in their productivity that justifies some attention to such matters.

POWER AND CABLING. We have already spoken (in Section 2.1) about the myriad problems of power wiring, and elsewhere about the various horrors of interference, static, and the like. Here, during the computer-room design phase, you have an opportunity to prevent many of the problems that have driven so many others to service bureaus.

The system, first, should be powered by a separate circuit that is used for nothing else. Coffee pots, copiers, fluorescent lights, and many other common devices can wreak havoc (please believe it: I once had to move a fluorescent fixture to another circuit because the system would very reliably crash whenever the light was turned off). This suggests the installation of a "sacred outlet" or two, with any unused sockets covered by those little plastic plugs that were originally designed to keep small fingers from becoming charred.

It also suggests a second circuit, on a different breaker from that of the machine, with convenience outlets all around the room. Operators of the system will have accessories such as hexadecimal calculators, radios, and swivel lamps, and it is best to keep them all away from the computer's private source of energy. Also remember that service personnel will need to plug in oscilloscopes and logic analyzers, and that janitorial folk will have need of power for such famous noise generators as buffers and vacuum cleaners.

We mention power wiring in this discussion about juggling paper cutouts to devise a good layout because your hands may already be tied by existing outlet placement. Since it is very much in your interest to keep the length of power cables to a minimum, the locations of these outlets can become annoyingly significant in computer room design.

The other cable-related item of note involves the data and signal wires that interconnect the various units of your system. In the case of the CRT terminal, cabling is probably noncritical: it is very likely a serial (RS-232) communications link, quite capable of trouble-free operation over hundreds of feet. Disk drives, however, and the occasional printer (like mine) that depends on parallel communication with the central processing unit (CPU), are a different matter. High-speed data communication suffers mightily when the length of the cable exceeds a few feet, and the manufacturer of your equipment may provide you with some rather severe constraints.

It becomes interesting, you see. The printer must be far away from the computer because of noise and need for easy rear access, but it must be close because of cable length restrictions and the need for operator convenience.

Oh yes—make sure that cables don't cross areas of the floor that carry human traffic, and that data cables don't run alongside those that carry ac power.

- **TELEPHONES.** A telephone line should be considered a necessity in the computer room. That is obviously the case if an acoustic coupler or direct-connect modem is going to be used for data communication with another machine. Even though your need may not be immediate, put one in anyway. Sooner or later, you are going to be talking with the factory about some system irregularity, and the disembodied voice on the other end of the line is going to ask you to enter some obscure command on the console and report the results. If this sort of thing becomes chronic, the act of running back and forth between your office and the computer room will eventually become a pain.

  As with most things, however, there's a catch. We already mentioned in our discussion of media care the unfortunate fact that a standard telephone ringer will disrupt the data on a nearby diskette. It would be best, therefore, to install the phone with a short cord that will prevent someone who may not know about that from placing the set on top of the disk drives, or next to the diskette box that contains original-issue software and all copies of work in progress. An alternative is to disconnect the bell in your desk phone, and install a wall ringer or other annunciating device.
- **MISCELLANEOUS.** By this time, the original straightforward layout of your paper cutouts has probably become tangled in a mire of conflicting requirements. We might as well throw in a few more.

  Room for expansion, first, is critical. Sometime down the road, you might need another printer, a second console, more file space, room for more people—or whatever. Businesses are rarely static, nor are the computers that serve them.

  Work space for the operator, as we mentioned, is very important. But there should be another table or two for long pondering sessions, field engineers' disassembly and repair of a unit, collating and its opposite, and temporary storage of work in progress. Such space also reduces the temptation to have lunch at the terminal.

  Somewhere within easy reach of the operator, there needs to be a big trash can. Is security a problem? You might also need a paper shredder.

  Where's the fire extinguisher?

Is sun shining in the window at any time of the year going to overheat the cabinets, blind the operator, warp the diskettes, or wash out the image on the CRT screen?

Are air-conditioning vents located such that they won't chill the human beings, but will adequately cool the hardware power hogs?

Is overhead lighting adequate, or will it cause glare on the screen and shadows on the work surface?

Is there hope for an ideal computer room?

So we have ten categories of contraints to deal with when trying to come up with a workable layout. Inevitably, there will be compromises, but up-front awareness of the foregoing, plus all the special requirements of your own installation, will decrease the frequency of future problems and changes, ensuring, meanwhile, a much smoother start-up process.

2.9 CLOSING NOTES

This chapter has focused, rather harshly perhaps, on the many environmental problems facing even a small computer system. Few would question extensive precautions in a large data-processing shop, but, probably because of the "appliance" nature of so many microcomputer systems, most people ignore the very similar requirements of the under-$10,000 machines.

It is very easy to become complacent with a computer's reliability when months and even years pass with little or no trouble. But many of the problems we described here are time bombs—a bit of grit in a diskette here, some thermal stress there—and ignoring them may eventually cause data loss.

A good, solid installation is the first step, but the second step is a human one. All people who are involved in any way with the machine should be familiarized not only with operational procedures but also with the principles we have discussed. One careless touch of a diskette's magnetic surface can wipe out a text file two years later.

But now, with this grim catalog of difficulties behind us, let's look to more complex matters. Once the system is installed, how can we keep it running smoothly?

3

Maintenance

3.0 INTRODUCTION

"Forget all this talk about reliability: if it plugs in, it's trouble."

These were the words of one seasoned industry observer when he was asked about hardware dependability. Although this may be unnecessarily cynical, there is unfortunately a measure of truth to his comment.

The compensating factor is that with an organized and conscientious maintenance program, a system manager can hold the occurrences of computer failure to a minimum and lessen the severity of the occasional "crash." But doing this involves more than making monthly payments on a maintenance contract. The more closely involved you are with the critical aspects of the machine, the more likely you will be to keep them under control and recognize impending problems before they become catastrophic.

System maintenance is an unglamorous aspect of computerization, but it can pay off handsomely. Let's first explore some preventive measures and then take a look at what can be done when failure occurs.

3.1 AN OUNCE OF PREVENTION . . .

Taking regular steps to prevent system failure is one of the secrets to successful computer use, from the most massive behemoths of IBM and Honeywell to the under $1000 machines that are popping up in homes around the world. Much in the preventive category is suggested by the environmental considerations highlighted in Chapter 2: proper thermal environment, clean work areas, and so on. But there are other things that should be done. The first step is the creation of a *preventive maintenance* (PM) schedule.

In Chapter 8 we will be talking about the paperwork associated with a small computer system, and one of the areas that shall receive ample mention is that of record keeping on the behavior of the system itself. The PM schedule fits here, together with a maintenance log, a questions and problems list, and a file of diagnostic procedures.

Establishing the PM schedule is not difficult, and depends on the details of your system. Following are loose recommendations concerning the attention that should be paid periodically to different machine components.

3.1.1 The Central Processing Unit

Containing, hopefully, no moving parts except for a cooling fan, the CPU should require little in the way of preventive maintenance. The exceptions involve the fan itself and other system components that may occupy the same cabinet as the computer—in particular, the disk drives.

Fan-cooling an equipment enclosure is an often-necessary evil. Ideally, the sensitive circuitry of a computer could be tucked away forever in a hermetically sealed black box, interconnected with the rest of the universe via appropriate power and data cables. This would keep dust and humidity out, as well as stray paper clips and airborne conductive carbon fibers.

The reality of the situation is, as discussed in Section 2.3, that the operation of any electronic circuitry involves a certain amount of inefficiency, which translates into power losses taking the form of heat. In a thermally closed space, this heat can build up to the point where it begins having a negative effect on the equipment, especially under conditions of elevated ambient temperature (which aren't limited to hard-core industrial environments—a desktop computer sitting in the sun can die just as easily). There are a variety of design alternatives available to rid the box of this heat, ranging from dependence on natural convection to the inclusion of miniature air conditioners. The typical small system falls somewhere in the middle, with a 4-inch cooling fan located in the back of the cabinet.In normal environments, this totally solves the problem. Excess heat is simply carried away in the continuous flow of air. This flow of air, however, raises the specter of contamination.

The typical office presents some surprisingly dirty conditions, a fact that might strike you rather abruptly when you open a piece of fan-cooled equipment and find it literally caked with greasy, inky dirt. The handling of continuous forms raises a lot of paper dust, and all the other stuff in the air that normally settles in an even layer over the entire office is briskly deposited inside a machine by any kind of active air mover. Some system components, such as the printed circuit boards comprising the processor itself, are relatively immune to this and can get quite grimy before negative effects are observed. Others, such as the disk drives that are normally mounted in the same cabinet, are not so lucky. It is very common to find a good thermal design that depends, for some of its cooling, upon air that is actually drawn into the cabinet through the openings in a pair of floppy disk drives!

Some designs take a more aggressive approach, with the inclusion of a filter adjacent to the fan. This appears on the surface to solve the entire problem, but it does so at the expense of another: if the filter becomes dirty enough to block the airflow, then we're right back where we started—to a closed space on the verge of overheating.

It is the task of a good preventive maintenance program to forestall the various forms of doom suggested by the foregoing, preferably by keeping the enclosure's interior and the filter, if provided, clean. While cleaning the interior of the unplugged machine with a soft brush (a paintbrush works well) and a vacuum cleaner, it is also a good idea to visually inspect the "seating" of circuit boards in their sockets and the general condition of cabling and other components. The latter items should never need attention, but occasionally the cumulative effects of vibration (or shipping) can lead to failure of a purely mechanical nature.

It is worth pointing out that a somewhat valid school of thought on the subject of PM states that "if it works; don't mess with it." Although it is true that the physical handling of equipment necessary to perform these procedures can, itself, cause problems, it is probably safe to observe that such cases are a minority. Equipment cooling, in particular, can suffer from benign neglect, and it's surely best to get that stray staple off the "motherboard" before it shorts the 12 volt power supply to one of the data lines.

3.1.2 The Disk Drives

Although disks are generally included in the same box with the computer proper, we give them their own dedicated discussion. It is probably safe to observe that disk drives and their media are the single most troublesome components in the small-system world.

This would not be corroborated by drive manufacturers, of course, but it is easy to see why it is true. Nearly everything else in the machine is safely "digital"—with the voltage at every point unambiguously representing either a "1" or a "0". Even printers, terminals, and modems, which depart from this simplified reality at their points of interface with the real world, generally do so in a relatively "solid" fashion.

Disk drives, however, must magically install and extract error-free data at accurately located points on a piece of rotating media. With double-density, double-sided, and double-tracking operation, we're talking about bits packed together about seven times as closely as the tiny dots that make up the photographs reproduced in this book—and errors of a single bit can have sweeping consequences.

This is even more severe in the world of hard disks (winchesters), but those are generally packaged in their own sealed enclosures, reducing the extent of potential environmental abuse. Floppies, on the other hand, are commonly treated with disrespect; many advertisements for computers even show naked diskettes lying on the surface of a desk. Consider the size of the average speck of dust.

All sorts of evil things can happen to disk drives. They can get dirty (causing *read* or *write errors*), they can be knocked out of alignment (making track-to-track positioning inaccurate and causing *seek errors*), or they can develop irregularities in their hubs (crunching the media and causing *track 0 errors)*.

A good number of problems can be avoided through the application of careful PM procedures. The most obvious task is simply keeping the heads clean, best accomplished with the occasional and careful use of cleaning disks. The job can also be done tolerably well with long cotton swabs and isopropyl alcohol, although this may require some disassembly.

The other standard item in the drive-maintainer's repertoire is alignment. To understand why this is a problem, we need to talk for a moment about the arrangement of data on a disk.

Ensconced within the lined confines of the square jacket is a circular piece of magnetic medium, not unlike that found (in the form of a long, skinny strip) inside an audio cassette. Set into rotation by the drive, which grips it around the center hole with a hub, it presents an exposed moving radial surface through the slot in the jacket.

The primary mechanical job of the disk drive is the accurate positioning of a head assembly to some point along that strip. At any given position, a *track* can be said to exist—something that could be made quite visible as a circular groove on the disk if the head is poorly made, or dirty enough to score the oxide coating. This happens.

The number of tracks varies, but on an average 8-inch floppy there are 77. Each track is broken up into some number of *sectors,* which are little segments of a circle that each contain a known amount of data. The CP/M operating system traditionally likes sectors of 128 bytes, but there is nothing sacred about this figure. In addition to the data recorded in each sector, there is also *header* information that relates positional data to the system and also contains some error-checking codes.

The problem introduced by misalignment is the failure of the drive to accurately position the head on a prerecorded track. This causes errors, which can be profound enough to render the drive unusable. Most often, the problem will be observed when attempting to read either a disk that was formatted (a process that writes the headers) on another drive, or one that was formatted on the same drive long enough ago that aging effects have changed its alignment.

This problem can be sneaky. Imagine: you carefully follow all the backup procedures to be described later in this book, creating a sacred master disk and periodic copies of your data, and storing them off-site to prevent catastrophe in the event of a fire or other sweeping loss. On a day-to-day basis, you read and write data to and from all your working disks as the business flows smoothly. You have no problems.

But one day, a particularly critical working disk develops an error in its directory area, rendering it useless. You grumble and complain, but aren't really too upset because you have a copy of the same thing stored elsewhere. You go get it.

After inserting it into the drive and initiating a "copy" procedure, however, you get a *seek error* message on the terminal. This persists no matter what you do, and it suddenly becomes clear that you have a real problem. The system is down.

How could a disk fail like that, just sitting in its envelope? It probably didn't. Far more likely is the fact that your drives have been slowly drifting out of alignment over the months (years?), but the problem was never manifested because you were continually updating disks throughout the gradual change. Old disks were discarded, new disks were created, and your volatile data propagated through the system without any difficulty—until it was time to use a disk that was recorded back at the beginning. The discrepancy—the total of all alignment changes during that interval—was just too much for the system to bear. Seek error.

The way to avoid all this is to keep the drives aligned. Unfortunately, this is a relatively distasteful technical procedure that may be difficult or impossible for most business system users. In essence, it involves inserting a special *alignment disk,* containing signals recorded just on either side of the center track, then making fine adjustments in the position of the head and stepper motor assembly until the "read" signals seen on an oscilloscope are properly balanced. One of these days, maybe some forward-looking drive manufacturer will include in the control logic of each unit a built-in alignment circuit, which lights a light-emitting diode (LED) on the board when the adjustment is correct. It would be trivial and would save a lot of trouble.

Until then, however, you are stuck with the options of waiting for trouble or periodically taking the drives to your local computer store for a tune-up. Either method is crude, and this points back to our opening discussion about the intrinsic flakiness of anything that depends on critical mechanical positioning and microvolt-level signals to perform a central and indispensable function in a computer system. The obsolescence of the floppy disk will lend a major boost of a small-system technology.

It *will* happen, perhaps with magnetic bubbles or super-high-density random access memory (RAM) that can provide the same data storage function as disks but with higher speed, no moving parts, and a fraction of the space. At this writing, unfortunately, such promising technologies as this are still either experimental or too expensive.

3.1.3 The CRT Terminal

Like the CPU, the CRT terminal is free of moving parts (those always cause trouble). To offset this, it has a high-voltage section. Even so, a well-designed unit should be very reliable and, with the exception of occasional cleaning, should only rarely require service.

It can probably be said of computer equipment in general that the most likely sites of failure are those that involve interconnection with the outside world. In the case of the CRT, there are three: the keyboard, the data link to the computer, and the power line. Of those, it is the keyboard that suffers the most abuse.

Still, there's not much that can be done from a preventive maintenance standpoint except, perhaps, giving the unit a thorough cleaning. The same soft brush that was employed in Section 3.1.1 to chase the dust from the circuit boards can be employed to clean the crevices between the rows of keys, and a soft, moist cloth can be applied to the rest of the unit to spruce it up a bit. Like a car, a terminal seems to undergo a psychological improvement in performance when it is clean.

There may be something to that. If your personnel have a benign attitude toward a nice-looking system, perhaps they will treat it more gently than they would a dirty, tattered machine littered with taped-on notes and bearing a three-year accumulation of fingerprints, cigarette smoke deposits, and general crud. This would class the basically unrelated operation of cleaning the cabinets right up there with preventive maintenance, wouldn't it?

3.1.4 The Printer

Second only to the disk drives in troublemaking potential, printers involve a variety of PM requirements. Much of this is traceable to the fact that they contain moving parts, the very things that make automobiles a never-ending pain.

Not only does this collection of moving parts suggest the need for lubrication and adjustment, but it is also subject to more physical abuse than any other part of a computer system (except, again, for the unfortunate keyboards of some particularly macho users). It must handle ream after ream of dusty paper, withstand the static discharge and mechanical stress of frequent handling, and survive the vibration of its own operation. A Diablo printer (daisy-wheel) that I used without the slightest mishap for years addressed these problems with design features not found in many of the new, low-cost models: solid circuit-board mounting, carefully planned airflow, roller bearings, conservative component specifications—in short, it was built somewhat like a tank. It matched the CPU board for reliability, a real accomplishment for anything with moving parts and doomed to suffer extensive human contact. But that's not typical.

Printers require more regular attention than most other parts of the system, depending on the complexity of the mechanism. Old ASR 33 Teletypes, standards in the industry for years, needed to be dunked in a large vat of lubricant periodically and "tweaked" by an experienced technician to continue operating properly. The new breed of low-cost matrix printers, on the other hand, should require very little beyond periodic cleaning and occasional lubrication of the linear bearings upon which the head assembly glides.

It is a good idea to keep certain accessories on hand—possibly in the same drawer with the head-cleaning kit for your disk drives and the random spare parts that will inevitably accumulate. For daisy-wheel printers, this would certainly include a spare wheel or two (although the stalwart Diablo celebrated above plowed through four years' worth of reasonably heavy use without so much as breaking a character tine), as well as a tube of the recommended lubricant (check the manual). For matrix types, the spares inventory might include a print head, now that the industry has finally matured enough to allow easy field replacement. Early matrix printer heads cost over $200 and were considered exotic components.

The key PM activity with printers, again, is cleaning. A considerable load of dust and little round pieces of paper that once occupied the spaces reserved for tractor-feed sprockets will accumulate inside the machine, eventually contributing to the likelihood of paper jamming and overheating. The platen should be removed periodically to allow a check for stray garbage that could interfere with proper paper movement—in particular, gummed labels that didn't feed properly and small items dropped into the machine over its normal use. For general printer cleaning, a portable vacuum cleaner is a big help.

The printer, especially if it is a large, complex, and expensive model (as opposed to the low-cost units that have proliferated of late), is a prime candidate for a maintenance contract if you are somewhat uneasy about digging in there now and again to apply a drop of oil or tighten a screw. Refer to Section 3.3 for some of the trade-offs accompanying this.

3.1.5 The System as a Whole

As in a close human relationship, a "super-identity" tends to develop when individual machines operate in close cooperation. There's the computer, the CRT, the printer, the modem—and then there's the whole system. Fused into what we hope is some kind of cohesive whole through implementation of intelligently designed software, the system represents a "meta-level" of operation that is something more than the simple sum of its parts.

Figure 3-1 The IBM Personal Computer. (Courtesy of IBM.)

The effects of this on equipment maintenance are many. First, the close involvement of so many components in any specific operation makes isolation of potential trouble difficult. Second, there are a few parts of the system that cannot be associated with any of the items we have discussed so far, but which must receive at least as much attention during PM checks.

Cables, for example, are frequent sources of trouble. Charged with the thankless task of shuttling data back and forth among the processor and its peripherals, they are generally wadded into bundles together with power cords in the dusty space behind a desk. They are tugged on when equipment is moved, walked on, tripped over, and tied in knots. The connectors that terminate them are stressed when unplugged with a yank on the wire, and they are often left to dangle from the backs of machines without benefit of the screws that are designed to hold them securely in place.

Any preventive maintenance checks should, without fail, include a comprehensive examination of the cabling. While running the printer, wiggle both ends of the cable that connects it to the computer. Any "burps" in the printing can be attributed to an intermittent connection, something that should be located and repaired before it causes the endless headaches of which it is capable. Similarly test the one going to the CRT and any other peripherals.

As mentioned in Chapter 2, some cables are very susceptible to noise pickup from nearby power wiring—in particular, those that carry parallel data (such as "Centronics-style" printer interfaces). These should be checked for clean routing, and if they are found to be tangled with everything else in that no-man's-land behind the desk, you might profit from taking a moment to tape them to a surface away from all the rest.

Power wires, as well, fall into this "meta" category. While checking the integrity of data cables, make sure that power plugs are well seated in their sockets and out of the way of feet.

The other "glue" that ties everything together is, of course, the software. It is difficult to think in terms of "preventive maintenance" when discussing software, but an overall operational check of the system is not a bad idea. In fact, a well-written diagnostic package (some of which have appeared on the market under names such as SHAKEDOWN) cannot only simplify the periodic PM checks but help home in on specific problems as well. If you don't have access to such a program, a sequence of operations that vigorously exercises all parts of the system may be used in its stead, such as a disk-to-disk copy followed by some extensive CRT activity and the printing of a file that calls for all the special features your printer has to offer.

3.2 . . . A POUND OF CURE

It would be worthwhile to note at this point that some documentation should be generated to tie together all the maintenance-related activities.

3.2.1 The Maintenance Log

We mentioned at the beginning of Section 3.1 the establishment of a preventive maintenance schedule. A good place to keep this is in a *maintenance log,* which can be used to tie together all information connected with the performance and repair of your system. In format, it can be as simple as a dedicated notebook, kept in a specified place, in which all persons involved with the machine are directed to note glitches, failures, fixes, needed components, suspicious behavior, and PM activity.

This is a tremendous help, and it is hard to imagine a successful small-system installation without at least a rudimentary version of this idea. It allows a pattern of irregularities to be observed over a period of time, hopefully yielding a regularity. It provides a means of recording the "fix" applied to a particular problem, probably rendering diagnosis and repair much easier the next time. It is a gold mine of information for a service technician, who frequently arrives at a customer's site only to hear something like, "it quit a couple of hours ago, but we reset it and it's been fine ever since." If examination of the maintenance log reveals a pattern of such behavior, it might be easier to correlate it with certain types of operations, certain times of day, or certain environmental conditions.

A typical log entry made after a random failure might read, "September 25, 1983—4:25 PM: Drive B started doing retries during text file save onto disk #58. CRT displayed SEEK ERROR message. I hit RETURN to make it try again, and it worked OK.—Steve."

This bit of information is nothing to write home about, but if it becomes part of a pattern of similar behavior, it probably indicates that there is a drive alignment problem, or, if disk 58 always seems to be involved, a media problem. In any case, collecting the observations of all concerned in one location will go a long way toward the rapid identification of trouble spots.

3.2.2 Crash!

Preventive maintenance and good record keeping notwithstanding, the system is quite capable of failing without so much as a microsecond's notice.

Your data-processing activities can be brought to an abrupt halt, with no indication of the time at which you can plan to resume operation.

This raises the specter of late payroll, missed deadlines, lost files, angry customers, misplaced shipments, and just about any other problem you can imagine that could be attributed to a sick computer. When the abrupt interruption of business activity is considered, it might even be justifiable to think in terms of acquiring backup hardware at whatever level is suggested by the *mean time between failures* (MTBFs) of the units involved. A spare disk drive, for example, makes more sense than a spare modem.

Downtime can be expensive. In my own operation, centered primarily around word processing for the writing profession, downtime is difficult to measure in dollars and cents—but it is still catastrophic. Work in progress lies, inaccessible, in a box of 100 or so floppies, and the creative urge wilts when confronted with the mechanical and wholly unaesthetic alternative known as the typewriter. Still, as long as I have been careful to produce a printed copy of everything, I am theoretically only inconvenienced.

The problem is worse for a business whose day-to-day activity is totally dependent on the machine. A medical clinic, for example, might use the system to house patient histories, drug and supply inventories, billing information, Medicare records, and payroll data. If their system dies, you can bet that someone is going to be more than frustrated. For this reason, the subject of equipment maintenance is apt to be a sensitive one in some circles.

In the best of all possible worlds, a system failure would be invisible to the user; this is, in fact, quite possible for certain types of problems. Modern high-density memory boards, for example, are more and more commonly being built with error detection and correction circuitry that single-handedly takes care of the glitches and "soft errors" caused by such things as stray alpha particles and static. But more sweeping failures, such as the incineration of a CPU board, are less likely to be fixable through an automatic and invisible operation.

The normal response to a failure is a human one: curse a bit, denounce the vendor, blame whoever was on the machine at the time, then try to make it work. The best approach to the latter is the following six-step sequence:

1. See if you can reliably reproduce the failure. At first glance, a failure would seem to be something to avoid (and that is certainly the case if the problem is the destruction of diskettes!), but the ability to repeatedly make the problem occur is the first step in locating it. Start by recreating the exact scenario that spawned the problem, then try variations and simplifications of that until you begin to observe a very specific cause-

and-effect relationship. This will not only make the following steps easier, but will be of considerable value if you end up on the phone to the manufacturer or a service organization.

2. Isolate the cause of the problem (which may have already become obvious from the first step). If the printer is producing garbage instead of five-year plans, for example, try printing a text file. If it is still garbage, try sending the console input directly to the printer. Still bad? If the printer has a self-test function, perform it. At this point, you will be able to state with certainty that the problem is either in the printer, or that it is somewhere between that and the most primitive levels of the processor. You can stop worrying about the integrity of your files.
3. Physically examine the suspect hardware. You may quickly discover a loose cable, a charred component, a stray bit of metallic debris, or a jammed mechanical assembly, and the problem is located. On the other hand, you may find nothing extraordinary; many failures are quite invisible although every bit as severe.
4. If the problem is one of unexplained "flakiness" or mysterious refusal to operate, you might try turning off the power, waiting a moment, then turning it on again. (This is subject to all sorts of exceptions: There's little point in this if the problem is manifested by smoke, and in certain cases, just hitting the RESET switch is adequate.) Power cycles, although themselves a possible source of difficulty, represent a return to the most basic level of machine operation. If the processor is simply off "chasing geese" in high memory somewhere, hitting the RESET button may be enough. But some devices, like this CRT I'm using, are capable of becoming so confused that a power cycle is necessary to restore normal operation. The problem with turning the machine off and on that I alluded to above is the thermal stress involved: Like light bulbs, computers are most likely to fail when they are first turned on. For this reason, I recommend avoiding exuberant use of the power switch if something else can do the same job. (Also bear in mind that in most systems, a power cycle replaces existing memory contents with random garbage. This may not always be advisable from a recovery standpoint—*think* first.)
5. Consult the manual. At this point, assuming that the machine is still dead, it is time to do some serious investigating. Drag out the manual on the affected unit, and locate the troubleshooting guide. This lists a set of checks that can be performed by the user without any special equipment, and that should definitely be performed before an expensive service call is ordered. Again referring to this CRT, for example, I note in the "Troubleshooting Checklist" eleven specific checks, including

the power cable, fuses, interface cables, and setting of the contrast control. This all sounds trivial, but it is easy to panic when the heat is on and then suffer extreme embarrassment when the $75 an hour service technician walks over to the machine, pushes in the circuit breaker, and hands you a bill for his one-hour minimum, plus travel time and a zone adder.

6. OK. *Now* you can call for help—or replace the offending machine with an in-house spare if you are lucky enough to have one. If a service call is taking place, be sure to deliver as much information about the problem over the phone to increase the odds that whoever visits will have the appropriate replacements in hand. Or if you are not in a position to invoke the services of an itinerant technician, you can show up at the computer store with an ailing machine under your arm, hoping for a quick fix.

The closing point above bears closer examination. How critical is your operation? Critical enough that the downtime and inconvenience represented by the need to drive a bad unit to a repair facility is unacceptable?

This is one of the arguments for selecting a machine in the first place that is elegible for a maintenance contract. This automatically limits your options to those of the "classier" and more expensive variety, but that can be justified anyway by a sufficiently critical installation. So let's look deeper into the subject of maintenance contracts, considering warranties in the process.

3.3 CONTRACT SUPPORT

A typical maintenance contract on a piece of equipment will stipulate a monthly payment that (once the warranty period expires) is a function of the overall hardware cost of the equipment to be covered. On a device such as a CRT terminal, this may run on the order of 25% per year (a $1200 terminal would thus cost $25 per month). A full system, on the other hand, should run not much more than 15% or so.

The cost of a maintenance contract varies with the amount (and speed) of service to be provided. Digital Equipment Corporation supports its line of small business systems with three types of service: "Basic," which on a system quoted at $9495 costs 13% of that per year; "Basic plus 24-hour toll-free number," which costs 14.5% per year; and "Four-hour guaranteed response," which costs 16.3%. The first option buys the customer "standard" service on a "first come, first served" basis, the second adds a WATS line for technical help (a large percentage of service calls can be taken care of over the phone by a sufficiently competent technician), and the third assures the user that the maximum wait for a technician will be four hours.

The maintenace contract that you sign with a system vendor will include a number of restrictions and limitations, largely designed to cover his proverbial posterior. Let's breeze through a plain-English paraphrase of a typical contract.

- **SCHEDULE OF EQUIPMENT TO BE COVERED.** The first item in the agreement specifies the models and serial numbers of the equipment involved, and spells out the corresponding charges, together with any warranty period during which the charges are waived.
- **SERVICES TO BE PERFORMED.** The first block of boilerplate (by the way, did you know that the reason legalese is traditionally so wordy is that lawyers, once upon a time, were paid by the word?) is involved with the services to be performed on your equipment, and the limitations of same. It stipulates, for example, that the vendor has the right to perform periodic inspections and appropriate PM, and that they have full and free access to the equipment during normal business hours. It goes on to describe the procedures by which service calls are handled: basically identifying the times of day during which they will respond and noting that off-hours work can be performed at the vendor's prevailing rates. Then come the disclaimers and limitations. You're on your own if the problems result from catastrophe, accident, neglect, abuse, misuse, power problems, operator error, data communications failure, connected equipment not provided by the vendor, or any cause other than ordinary use. They won't fix anything not noted in the schedule of equipment to be covered, nor will they cover things that *are* if they have been modified in any way. The contract does not cover installation or relocation, supplies, rebuilding, or overhauling.

  Here's a tough one: the contract then states that if the equipment is found to be working properly when a service technician arrives in response to your call, his visit will be charged at the then-prevailing rates. (Think twice before calling.)

  Finally, the section on limitations points out that the vendor may, if the equipment is not presently covered by a maintenance contract, perform an initial inspection that will be chargeable to the customer.
- **CHARGES.** This obbligato paragraph simply points out that service, if not paid for, shall cease.
- **WARRANTY.** The vendor doesn't make promises he can't keep. The company "warrants that the services performed hereunder will be performed in a workmanlike manner in accordance with reasonable

commercial standards." A following statement points out that the preceding statement is in lieu of all other warranties expressed or implied, including merchantability, fitness for a particular use, or any other matter.

- **EXCUSED PERFORMANCE.** As if the vendor were not already protected enough from undue exposure, this entertaining paragraph states that it (or its contractors) cannot be held liable for any loss or damage resulting from a failure to provide service for causes beyond its control, "including, without limiting the generality of the foregoing, acts of God, unanticipated natural phenomena, acts of the Customer, governmental action, fire, strikes, war, weather, wrecks or delays in transportation, priorities or preferences given orders for U.S. government procurement, and inability to obtain labor or materials."
- **TERM.** This paragraph specifies the period of time covered by the agreement, the ways in which it can be terminated, and the rights of the vendor in the event of the customer's bankruptcy or insolvency.
- **MISCELLANEOUS.** A final comment notes that this agreement constitutes the entire agreement (lest any doubt remain).

Once such an agreement has been executed between you and your system vendor (or the independent provider of maintenance service), you are essentially insured against expensive, unanticipated repair bills, assuming, of course, that you comply with the various restrictions noted above. Most of them sound academic, but one item in particular deserves additional mention.

There will probably be, sooner or later, a strong temptation to modify your system. This can consist of something as innocent as the insertion of a special-function circuit board (such as a real-time clock or speech synthesizer) made by a different manufacturer, or it may involve actual equipment modification that alleviates some particularly annoying deficiency. In either case, you risk violation of your maintenance contract.

I witnessed one sad case in a medium-sized accounting firm located in America's heartland. The computer, now mercifully out of production, was able to accommodate multiple users through the rather quaint mechanism of isolated fields of memory for each user, plus a common area accessible to all of them. The architecture of the machine placed serious restrictions on interuser communication outside certain prescribed methods, and this frequently led to frustration on the part of customers who could almost, but not quite, perform something elegant such as a file transfer directly from one user to another. The system manager was convinced that he could "compute the world"—if only the restriction was lifted.

A helpful consultant took one look at the logic of the machine, and announced to everyone's surprise that the addition of one switch, nothing more, would do the job. A switch was hastily procured and mounted on the cabinet, and three wires were run to appropriate spots inside the machine (all it did was swap the source of a "memory select" signal between users). It worked beautifully; everyone was happy.

Things remained more or less idyllic until something (quite unrelated) broke. The field engineer showed up armed with tool kit, oscilloscope, and spare circuit boards, saw the switch on the front panel, and froze. "What the hell is *that?*" he finally managed to blurt out.

"Oh, that's just our *memswap* switch," the manager replied jovially. "Wanna see it work?"

"Can I use your phone?"

Thus ensued a brief chat between the field engineer and his manager, during which the information was relayed that the firm had tampered with the system's hardware. He hung up the phone, and heading for the door, said, "Sorry, my boss says you're on your own. We're not allowed to service modified systems." Another user is orphaned.

You might be thinking, "Ah, that was his fault. *I'll* never have occasion to do that sort of thing." Probably not. But you might be tempted, especially if you are acquiring a system that uses one of the popular bus structures such as the S-100. There's a wealth of clever accessories that can be added to a stock machine, usually with a minimum of difficulty, and some of them can dramatically enhance the system's value. But beware of snags with your service contract.

Let's close out this chapter with a few tales, then move on to more catastrophic matters than mere hardware failure.

3.4 A FEW RANDOM WAR STORIES

One of the perennial features of the computer business is the entertaining diversity of tales that arise from system problems. Eavesdrop on a gathering of field engineers sometime; the stories you'll hear will curl your hair.

- **HIGH VOLTAGE.** A friend of mine, for example, once had occasion to answer a frantic service call from a company whose system had inexplicably died, with a lot of smoke. He showed up, replaced the power supply and two charred circuit boards, then headed out the door to catch a plane.

  "Wait!" someone called after him. "It just did it again!" He ran back in, hoping to catch the cause of the problem, but found exactly the same thing. He implemented an identical fix, then settled in to wait for a recurrence with one unblinking eye focused on the screen of an oscilloscope that was monitoring the power supply. He waited.

And waited. After a few hours of this, he began to conclude that the problem had disappeared, so he packed up his things and filled out a service report. "Mind if I run a copy of this?" he asked.

He walked over to the new copier that the company had recently purchased, inserted the document, and pressed START. The lights dimmed, and a cry from the computer room echoed down the hall. The copier? Aha!

A bit of investigation revealed the cause of the problem: the newly installed copier required 220 volts, and the lazy electrician who installed the machine simply brought in two conveniently located 110-volt lines to provide the power. One of them was the sacred line to the computer, and the effect of the copier's load, plus the out-of-phase wiring job and lack of a ground circuit, combined to hit the system with over 200 volts whenever the copier was activated. That was just too hot to handle.

- **THE 25-CENT PART—THE $25,000 PROBLEM.** This one could give a person bad dreams. A fairly robust business system began exhibiting rather antisocial behavior: it would fail without warning, only to come back up in about five minutes. This occurred with catastrophic frequency (every half-hour or so) and rendered the machine quite useless.

  Service technicians were called, of course, but no amount of component replacement appeared to have much effect. For fourteen days this went on, during which time the end of the month went by, leaving the customer in dire straits with *his* customers complaining bitterly about their unprocessed data (the owner of the system was an accounting service).

  Fourteen days. Engineers flew in from the plant, technicians flew in from regional offices, and a consultant even showed up from a local computer firm, armed with the latest in sophisticated test equipment. The system would fail, they'd swap a part, the system would go back up—then fail. But finally someone found the problem.

  A fuse. A 25-cent slow-blow fuse had developed the annoying characteristic of "opening" when it got hot, and closing again when it cooled off. The system behaved very much like a large, slow version of one of those blinking Christmas tree bulbs.

Needless to say, the president of the company was not too impressed when he found out that it was only a fuse. Heads, predictably, rolled.

- **PATTERN-SENSITIVE MEMORY.** Some problems are even more obscure. I'll spare you the grisly details, but an environmental control and energy management system custom-designed for a large university exhibited some strange behavior upon startup. One of the tasks it was supposed to perform was the alphabetical sort of about 500 blocks of data corresponding to monitored points around the campus (air-handling units, chillers, air temperature, etc.).

  It did this, but in the process it seemed to create some garbage data. The engineer who designed the machine came in, mulled over the program for a while, decided that it must be a hardware problem, and reached into the machine to swap the memory boards around. Just a hunch.

  Even to *his* surprise, the hunch was a good one. The problem changed when the memory was readdressed: Instead of creating garbage data, the system displayed the time on its screen as "G%aP.22B." The configuration of the boards was changed again, and the system wouldn't even run. It was changed yet again, and a certain type of alarm-reporting function stopped working.

  At this point, it was patently obvious that one of the five memory boards was bad. A spare was brought in and swapped, one at a time, with the originals, but although the problem kept changing, it never disappeared entirely. The customer was finally persuaded to buy a fresh set of boards. They didn't work right, either.

  The engineer, by this time somewhat less popular with his client, started digging through the software again, at last spending over a day "single-stepping" the machine and creating a detailed written trace of its operation. At last, the problem revealed itself: it was one little instruction in the program.

  It seems that the instruction, which determined when the sort operation would terminate, was allowing one extra swap of data fields to be performed. Since the system was out of data to swap at that point, the determination of which chunks of memory were going to be exchanged was a matter of some chance. It depended, in fact, on whatever random data happened to be in memory before the program was executed (indeed, he discovered that preloading memory with all zeros "solved" the problem). The reason different memory boards were having characteristic effects was simply due to the nature of the chips on which they were based: they generally tend to power-up with the same configuraton of bits each time.

- **THE DIGITAL BOAT ANCHOR.** Back in Chapter 2, I related a brief tale about a system plagued by relentless static problems. That wasn't *all* that plagued it, bad design being another source of endless difficulty.One particularly noteworthy fiasco occurred one afternoon when I was, unfortunately, the only representative of the vendor who happened to be within the range of a wrathful data-processing manager.

  The scenario was this: The customer, a large freight-handling company that controls a healthy percentage of the nation's barge traffic, routinely followed proper backup procedures to protect its considerable investment in ongoing barge data. Every day, the data base was copied from disk to one of three backup tapes, which were then stored in a fireproof safe. The tapes took turns receiving the daily dump, thus representing at any given time the status of all shipping during the last three days.

  One day, something "glitched" the files on disk (static, no doubt), and rather than try to dig around in many megabytes of data and fix all the problems, the data-processing manager decided to just clear the whole mess and recreate it from the most recent backup. Operators would be required to reenter the day's changes, but this was hardly prohibitive. The latest tape was fetched, mounted on the drive, and directed to play. Nothing. It was a blank tape.

  With a sinking feeling in the pit of his stomach, the manager called for the other two. Same thing: virgin tape. They might as well have been brand new, untouched by data as they were. Other file tapes were tried, and worked all right, but the backup tapes that now represented the company's only hope for recovery refused to yield so much as a bit. "*Why?*" he bellowed, catching me by the scruff of the neck. I could only commiserate.

  Considerable frenzied digging with an oscilloscope at last yielded the sad truth: the tape drive contained a hardware problem that caused it to write all zeros on the tape no matter what was being fed to it. Error-detection logic was, of course, supposed to catch such things, but the same problem that cleared the data also cleared the check bits in the "read-after-write" circuitry. The drive was telling the computer that everything was fine—keep on sending—but the data were just going to the proverbial "bit bucket."

  Many days of 24-hour effort were required to piece the data base together again, and no expletives were spared in denouncement of the vendor.

These tales just scratch the surface, and represent hardly a fraction of the problems that appear regularly in the computer world. But let's assume that you have a solid machine that is well supported by contractual maintenance support: Are you home free? If the software is good and the hardware never breaks, what could go wrong?

Let us now look at some problems of a more serious nature.

4

Catastrophe

4.0 INTRODUCTION

Throughout the foregoing chapters, we have spent more time discussing problems than successes. If you are new to this game, all this might be a trifle disconcerting, especially when you turn the page and find a chapter called "Catastrophe."

Well, we might as well get it out of the way. These *are* valid concerns: systems do die, vendors are sometimes a major pain to deal with, and yes, vandalism occurs. So do fires.

These catastrophic events are hardly unique to computer systems, of course; they are equally applicable to photocopiers, cars, and business in general. But the presence of an information-handling system changes the picture somewhat, since more than simple equipment replacement is involved. Let's consider some of the potential occurrences in this category, and the steps that can be taken "up front" to minimize their severity (or prevent them entirely).

4.1 ACCIDENTS AND NATURAL DISASTERS

Catastrophic problems can be broadly divided into two categories: those that are the result of somebody's deliberate actions and those that are not. In the latter category are such things as fires, floods, tornadoes, lightning damage, earthquakes, and human accidents such as coffee spills or dropping a machine. Let us dispense with these before we look at the problems that can be *really* expensive.

It is desirable at the onset of system acquisition to undertake some form of *risk analysis* (even if only of the "seat-of-the-pants" variety) in order to determine the amount of money and effort to be expended on loss prevention and recovery. It is tempting, especially in the small-system world, to ignore the problem and just plunk the box down in your office, but this attitude ignores the dependency on the computer that is likely to develop. It has been observed that a company of any size risks "corporate extinction" if it ignores protective measures and problems of site security.

Much of the rationale behind this lies not in the value of the equipment itself, which can usually be replaced with little trouble, but instead with the concentration of company information housed within it. This can range from business data (consider the effects of losing your accounts receivable files) to work in progress representing massive investments in human time. All this adds up to a very high value per square foot around your computer, be it big or small; one fire of only 650 square feet a few years ago resulted in a loss of over $4 million. And . . . it *can* happen here.

4.1.1 Fire

Since fire is the largest single catastrophe in the "accidents and natural disasters" category, it shall receive our emphasis. Most accidents are relatively local in scope, and can be minimized with careful computer room planning as outlined in Section 2.8. Most natural disasters occur without warning and are relatively impervious to protective measures (how do you put out an earthquake?).

Fire, on the other hand, is an ever-present threat that is sadly ignored by most people. Something as innocent as a paper jam or a dirty filter can cause combustion, and there is always the possibility of frayed wires, shorts, sudden equipment failures, liquid spills, lightning, arson, and the spread of a nearby fire already under way.

Determining the trade-off between the cost of protection and the cost of potential loss (multiplied by its probability) is the essence of risk analysis. Considering the economy of basic preventive measures, such analysis will inevitably yield a decision to invest in at least a smoke detector or two, a fire extinguisher, and some of the backup procedures to be described shortly.

The choice of a fire-extinguishing method is not as obvious as it sounds. It is well known, for example, that water sprinklers are not a particularly good choice for electrical fires, but even if the power is automatically shut off when they are activated, they have the disadvantage of causing extensive water damage. This can be much worse than the effect of the fire itself in some cases.

Foam extinguishers solve that problem neatly, and like sprinklers, are cheap and effective. But instead of causing extensive water damage, they cause extensive foam damage. The stuff is almost impossible to extract from the innards of equipment.

Dry chemical is about as bad: it crystallizes and binds to hot components.

Carbon dioxide types, on the other hand, swiftly and efficiently put out a fire without causing equipment damage. The main problem is that they tend to asphyxiate human beings by robbing them of oxygen, necessitating the sounding of an alarm 30 seconds or so before their activation to induce computer room personnel to depart. A second problem is thermal shock to system components: CO_2 is *cold.*

The delay problem can be critical, and suggests the use of the fifth alternative: Halon 1211 (Figure 4-1). Like carbon dioxide, this substance

Figure 4-1 Halon fire extinguishers are the only type considered safe for computer rooms. (Courtesy of Inmac.)

(hydrocarbon bromide) acts quickly without causing damage—but it is harmless to human beings (indeed, a standard trade-show demo involves a man in a glass booth holding a burning object, which quickly goes out upon release of the gas). This makes it the universal first choice for computer rooms. Halon extinguishers are available in sizes ranging from small hand-held units containing about 2.5 pounds, to giant "systems" meant for large-scale data centers. I recommend picking a unit of the appropriate size and making it a key fixture in your computer room. It's cheaper than the insurance that would be necessary to provide comparable protection.

Speaking of insurance, there comes a point whereon it is desirable to transfer some of the risk to an outside agency. Halon or no, some damage will occur if a fire takes place, and it is nice to have someone to call with hope of cash assistance. We will deal with this subject more thoroughly in Section 4.3.

4.1.2 Protect Yourself

All the Halon in the world, of course, won't bring back lost data, and we should spend some time discussing ways of covering yourself in the event of a catastrophic loss. You basically face two risks when extensive computer room damage is considered: loss of information, and loss of information-processing capability.

The first of these can be rather handily addressed with a backup protocol through which you periodically store copies of your critical files in some off-site location. I have found a safe-deposit box at the bank to be reasonably trouble-free, costing only $40 per year and easing my mind considerably about the loss of manuscripts and system software in the event of a disaster. This approach, as opposed to storage of diskettes at a friend's house or with another system user, prevents potential breaches of security through casual copying or outright theft.

Where business records are involved, this issue becomes doubly critical. Loss of financial data, accounts receivable, inventory records, and so on, can be thoroughly crippling. Implementing an off-site backup program may not only be good insurance, but essential to the life of your business.

Another approach is justified in some cases: telecommunicating your data periodically to a cooperating associate with compatible hardware. This lowers the cost of backup, enables it to be performed daily with a minimum of difficulty, and ensures that the media containing your records will still be readable if your system is destroyed. Indeed, this is the other problem we mentioned earlier—loss of information-processing capability.

If your system has been reduced to charred rubble, a handful of diskettes isn't much help unless you have some way to read them. Presumably, steps would be taken with all due haste to acquire a replacement, but this might have to wait for items to come into stock, custom work to be done, or insurance claims to be settled. In the meantime, operations have ground to a halt and frustrated your attempts to maintain some measure of continuity.

Why not associate yourself with one or more users of similar equipment in your area, forming something of a consortium dedicated to mutual backup and aid in the event of catastrophe? You are sure to have common interests anyway, and the assurance of "friendly" facilities if your system is down for any reason (including simple hardware failure—let's not dwell on disaster overmuch) can go a long way toward increasing your comfort with the gradual assumption of all company record keeping by the computer. Some firms, "computerized" for years, still maintain completely parallel manual accounting systems because of their lack of trust in the equipment. This is not entirely unreasonable where some brands of computer are concerned, but the technology hasn't exactly stood still, and there *are*, after all, better ways.

Anyway, establishment of a consortium as described will have the effect of providing both data and equipment backup, allowing a continuation of the information side of your business in the event of a problem. If you are a lone user of your particular brand of machine, a sufficiently friendly relationship with your vendor can have a similar effect.

4.2 HUMAN PROBLEMS: VANDALISM AND THEFT

The *real* problems with computers, of course, are related to security. Information crimes are so rampant in this technological society that the FBI now has a special division dedicated to the problem, ex-convicts who were incarcerated for computer-assisted theft now knock down respectable consulting fees helping companies avoid victimization, and every month or so there arrives in my mail announcement of another seminar on computer crime and data security. It must be a problem.

Before you skip ahead with complacent assurance that only big data-processing centers need bother themselves with such classic accoutrements as combination locks and password-protected files, take a few moments to think about the possible losses to *your* business if the wrong people were to obtain your records. If this yields only a shrug of your shoulders, try to imagine the potential damage that could be wrought by a disgruntled employee or by random vandalism. If even *this* isn't particularly unnerving, your use of the system is probably casual—and you may skip ahead.

Life, of course, is a tyranny of trade-offs, and the problem of microsystem security is a perfect example. Techniques exist that could render your operation so thoroughly impervious to assault and information theft that you could probably even sleep well with a computer full of proprietary data that are lusted after by the Other Side. You could build a windowless concrete building within a windowless concrete building, require three-level access control based on passwords, keys, and fingerprints, and transmit data only in encrypted form. You could implement a watchdog system that makes an unalterable audit trail of all activity, shred and incinerate listings, and vigorously prosecute even the most casual misappropriation of computer time.

But would much work get done? Would the costs of all these protective measures (in dollars and human time) negate the value to be derived from the computer itself? Would said costs, in fact, be greater than the potential losses if a breach of security *were* to occur?

Hence the trade-off. Somewhere in here, you must establish a list of potential security problems and rank them according to the product of their probability and severity. This should yield a reasonable prioritization, which can then be used to determine the amount of protection necessary. (It might be noted, for example, that the total destruction of your computer room by international terrorists, although unquestionably catastrophic, is not worthy of as much concern as the simple divulgence of employee records to others within the company.)

Whatever the outcome of this analysis, you should remember that there are operational costs associated with every security measure implemented. Even something as obvious as keeping confidential files separate from those of a casual nature requires diligent adherence to a set of protocols, lest the effect of the effort be lost in the confusion of daily operation.

This all boils down to the observation that some security risks are going to have to be accepted, since efforts to prevent them will unjustifiably delay work and interfere with personnel flow. As will be noted later in this chapter, a good risk-control program will start bringing insurance companies into the picture at about this point.

Let us spend a moment looking at the types of abuse to be found, then explore products and techniques that can help prevent them.

4.2.1 A Catalog of Abuses

The kinds of actions that fall within the realm of computer security problems range from the simple unauthorized use of system time for games to such distressing acts as "computer murder" and blackmail. Let's consider the possibilities.

- **INFORMATION THEFT.** Perhaps the most obvious misuse of a company's computer involves infiltration by someone whose objectives are not aligned with those of the firm. The potential impact of this is entirely a function of the information housed in the system—in my case, the risk is relatively low (might someone steal this manuscript and publish it under his own name?), but then, this is a relatively low-key system installation. But it is easy to imagine the effects of theft and subsequent sale of a manufacturing firm's customer list: the resulting erosion of market position could indirectly cost millions.

  Information theft occurs with astonishing frequency, in ways that might seem trivial to those involved. A big issue these days is *software piracy,* for example, where individual system owners innocently swap copies of licensed programs to save money. "Hey, I'll give you WordStar for a copy of that data base package you've been using." This is hardly fair to the guys who wrote the programs, and if your name is on the licensing agreement for a serial-numbered product that turns up in someone else's possession, you might find yourself with a lawsuit on your hands. The nature of this business is such that a lot of computer people are hobbyists as well, and if you are not the only one who has access to your system, it would be well to keep an eye on valuable software. Of course, it only takes a few seconds and a piece of blank medium to make a copy, so it is also a good idea to control the stock of diskettes—and to sign a "toothed" nondisclosure agreement with your employees.

  As we talk about information theft, it becomes clear that doing something about it is hard (Figure 4-2). Threats exist both inside and outside a company—with the former obviously much harder to control.

  One problem is invasion of privacy. If your machine houses medical records, personal financial data, or even routine employee information, it is subject to abuse by certain parties. Financial information about your company is not for public distribution, nor are sales data, inventory records, credit information, discount schedules, salaries, and the work in progress of your in-house programming staff.

  And leaks exist at many levels: information can pass out of your control through telecommunications, on stolen or copied media, and on discarded printouts. You are vulnerable to the actions of janitors, night watchmen, consultants, spies, secretaries, programmers, and bribed management personnel—for the profit motive is a strong one and someone with beady eyes on your precious data may not be averse to a payoff. Even something as innocent as on-line time can be "stolen" and used for anything from game playing to handling the data-processing needs of another firm.

Figure 4-2 Putting your diskettes in a fireproof safe under lock and key is one way to help you sleep better; this unit from Uarco will keep diskettes within their safe temperature limits even through a one-hour blaze at 1700°F. The bottom drawer similarly protects documentation. (Courtesy of Uarco Incorporated, 121 North Ninth Street, Dekalb, IL 60115.)

- **PECUNIARY THEFT.** The more traditional type of theft applies equally as well, but with a computerized twist. Many business systems are in a position that renders them choice avenues of access to money for clever thieves, and unfortunately, most system users are unaware of the potential risk they face. Information can be stolen and sold, but in some situations, money can be stolen directly.

  It is not common to speak of "white-collar crime" outside the world of big data-processing systems, but if anything, the small user is even more exposed than his large-scale counterparts. Few protective techniques are applied to systems that shuttle dollars among various accounts and issue payroll checks, and I have actually seen installations where a box of continuous-form company checks routinely sits behind the printer stand, with the software that handles disbursements resting in a binder full of floppies—in plain sight. A sufficiently brazen employee with very little imagination could embezzle a few thousand and be gone long before anybody noticed.

There are a number of methods for controlling the blatant or subtle misappropriation of funds, and we shall consider them shortly.

- **PROGRAMMER FRAUD.** This one is perhaps the most insidious of all: the use of special knowledge by a system's programmer to defraud the company. It applies equally well to both types of theft we have discussed so far.

  The problem here, of course, is that programmers—those noble souls without whom computers would sit inert like so much raw material—possess, by definition, the key to every program that flows from their fingertips. Sure, you can type in a secret password, but the programmer knows where in system memory the password is stored.

  Some programmer fraud is just for fun, such as the famous old trick called the "unknown glitch." A large business system would inexplicably interrupt its processing, print the message, "HI! I AM THE UNKNOWN GLITCH! CATCH ME IF YOU CAN."—and then resume operation quite normally. No amount of naive poking about could reveal the location of the trick code, for it relocated itself continually and kept the message string stored in encrypted form to avoid detection by a simple memory dump or scan.

  Unfortunately, fraud doesn't stop with this sort of fun. A disgruntled (or hungry) programmer might build in a "trap door" that will allow later undetected entry into the system and manipulation of the data therein. Or the phenomenon of "breakage" can be applied, where fractional parts of cents left over from calculations are shuttled off to a special account.

  If the programmer simply wants to cause damage, he (or she, of course) can quite easily include a bit of code in a program that will cause the company's system (or its customers' systems) to crash suddenly upon encountering a certain date or a specific dollar amount. One chap added an extra twist: before leaving the company he worked for, he patched the software of an applications job to self-destruct on his birthday the following year. A very discerning manager noted the coincidence and traced the problem to its source.

- **SABOTAGE AND VANDALISM.** Disgruntled employees, again, are probably the primary source of concern in this category. A small magnet concealed in someone's pocket can mysteriously destroy the data on disks held by his side, and a pin shoved into a data cable can drive people crazy in the attempt to find the problem. Liquids can have disastrous effects, ventilation holes can be covered, air conditioners can be shut off, physical equipment damage can be done—it's all very depressing. If you are paranoid by nature (or in a sensitive business) you can also worry about bomb threats and computer murders. As with abuses in the preceding categories, the problem lies in the strong concentration of value and vulnerability represented by a company's computer system.

Let's turn now to some of the things that can be done to prevent all this.

4.2.2 Security Techniques

A large percentage of the countermeasures that can be applied to the potential threats can be considered within the common sense category. It only makes sense that one shouldn't leave key files lying about, and anyone who leaves the computer unattended and unwatched is asking for trouble. Unfortunately, depending on such simple techniques for system security is not always sufficient.

As we have noted, the amount of money and effort that can justifiably be spent on security depends on the probability of a loss and its potential cost. Security is expensive. It would be pleasant if we could locate computers in solid concrete buildings with no doors or windows, subject all personnel to exhaustive screening, and ensure that no datum remains unencrypted for more than a few microseconds. But it would be difficult, in such an operational context, to get much work done. The art of risk management is in the determination of an appropriate balance between (as usual) cost and benefit.

Access control, for example, is subject to this trade-off. We already mentioned the "man trap" in Chapter 2, wherein a person desiring entry to the room must first find himself locked in an anteroom, subject to the scrutiny of a guard. For most microsystems, this is a bit much. The anteroom would probably be bigger than the computer room.

More reasonable in our context is an access control scheme that depends on one of three things: a person's knowledge (of a password or special code), his possessions (a key or magnetically encoded card), or his personal attributes (fingerprints, facial appearance, etc.). The latter, at this stage of the technology, still depends for accuracy on a human guard, since recognition systems that approach a reasonable level of reliability cost quite a bit more than the average small system.

The other two are quite useful in our context. Numerous combination locks are on the market, the best known of which is probably the Code-a-Sentry (Figure 4-3), and locks requiring the insertion of a badge are not hard to find. Then, of course, there's always the simple key type, probably

Figure 4-3 The Code-A-Sentry combination lock is a popular access-control device that can be reprogrammed at will with new combinations. (Courtesy of Inmac.)

quite sufficient unless the potential value of your information to someone else is such that acquisition and duplication of a key would be considered well worth the effort.

The important thing to remember, if you are taking access control seriously, is that it has to be enforced to be worth anything. I have seen highly secure doors propped open around the clock, "tailgaters" who pass through on someone else's key, and general casual attitudes brought about by months of complacency and business as usual. Only your own requirements can serve as a guide: if the need for security is great enough to justify some preventive measures, they should be kept in force throughout the life of the system.

The idea of access control applies at levels other than that of the computer room as a whole. Individual terminals can be equipped with keylocks, as can cabinets containing information-laden media. It is also a good idea to keep confidential files apart from those of a more "public" nature, and impose some measure of intimidation by clearly marking them as such. Casual copying can be inhibited with the subtle implication of legal action. Similar "psychological" control can also be exerted through the execution of strongly worded contracts with your employees and subcontractors, promising litigation in the event of disclosure or theft of company information.

Programs and data files can be equipped with locks, too. Known universally as *passwords,* they can prevent unauthorized access to sensitive information without placing an undue burden on either the system or its legal users (Figure 4-4). Most multiuser operating systems include password

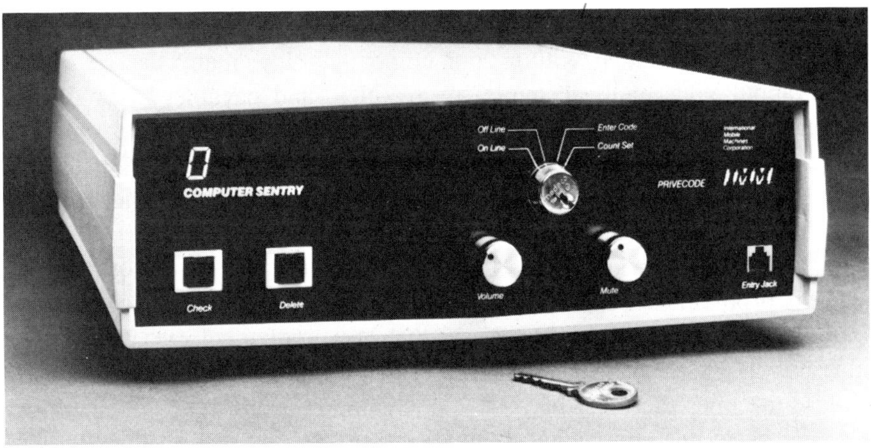

Figure 4-4 The Computer Sentry can stop unauthorized access before it starts by requiring the caller to enter a password (via either touch-tone or voice) before allowing the system's modem to respond. Offering a host of "front-end" security features, it can thwart even those who know your system passwords and sign-on procedures. (Courtesy of Computer Products Division, International Mobile Machines Corporation.)

identification of users as a standard feature, but this is relatively rare in the single-user world.

In any case, a password should be changed periodically to limit its proliferation, it shouldn't be obvious, and it should not, of couse, be printed or left on the terminal screen after entry by the user.

Some systems allow different user levels, or at least provide for one "privileged" user who can manipulate the system at a more intimate level than the others. This is worth investigating if your organization contains a "hacker" or two who may seize any opportunity to dig around in the file structure and try a few things (although not necessarily with the intent of fraud). A strict separation between user and supervisory levels will also have the effect of limiting the scope of operator error: some accidental key sequences can clear a whole disk in a second or two.

Wherever your information appears, it needs to be protected. This is as true of the trash can as it is of your disks: If someone can just retrieve a listing from the dumpster, why should he bother trying to get past your elaborate security system? Try to limit the proliferation of sensitive listings, and acquire a paper shredder if you have no choice.

A lot of this may seem quite melodramatic, conjuring cloak-and-dagger images of information spies lurking about your dumpster in the dead of night. It may sound quite absurd in the light of your application. But suppose that you are using the machine to develop some marketable software, and your competition acquires a listing of the code? Or suppose that your payroll records were circulated within your company? How many people should know about your bank accounts, receivables, and payables? About your patients, vendors, or clients? Should opposing counsel be able to produce copies of damaging legal correspondence? Do you want copies of that erotic novel you're writing after hours on the word processor to circulate without benefit of pseudonym?

I interject occasional reminders like this because it is common for security problems to be ignored or treated in an offhand manner. This section is most emphatically not a proposal that you implement every protective measure discussed; it is only a catalog of possibilities from which you should choose the ones that best fit your application.

So assuming, now, that methods are in place to restrict unauthorized access to the machine, its files, and printed listings, how can we carry it further to discourage or catch those who are more persistent?

One useful technique involves the *seeding* of confidential files with false information in a few places. You might, for example, add the name "Bolivar Shagnasty" to your customer list, with your own home address. If Bolivar ever receives anything other than authorized company correspondence, you have a pretty strong case against the originator of the mailing.

You can also encrypt files of this sort, although this raises processing overhead considerably. It's all a function of the degree of secrecy that you must maintain to feel safe.

One technique that should *always* be applied, especially in accounting systems, is the audit trail. Long a standard routine for noncomputerized accounting methods, this ongoing record of every change made to the books has helped many a business hone in on an embezzler or backtrack to find an error. If your accounting files are lost or destroyed, the most recent backup (you *do* have a backup, don't you?) is only a starting point: it must be brought up to date with a repeat of the entries that have occurred since the time it was made. The audit trail, just one of the necessary cross-checks, makes this easy.

Closely allied with this is another protocol that should be considered *de rigueur* in any money-handling system: a strict separation of duties. Depending on the size of your company, you should attempt to minimize the chances of embezzlement by employing different people to process incoming checks, manipulate inventory records, handle receivables and payables, and reconcile bank accounts. I have been stung: it was due to my gracious issuance of *carte blanche* to a very shrewd bookkeeper (who deftly logged 31 separate counts of fraud in a nine-day period before she became greedy and careless).

Periodic auditing of the system's data is not a bad idea either, now that the industry has been around long enough to produce auditors not terrified by the notion of a computer system that hosts the books. This, combined with the cross-checks and safeguards outlined above, should provide you with a considerable increase in confidence (something that is often shaken, even in experienced users, by the relative mystery of a system problem).

The only drawback to all this is that a sufficiently competent person can circumvent every preventive measure you implement. A sly programmer, as noted in the preceding section, can build trapdoors into your software that allow money or information to be extracted at will, and even without this, someone who knows a lot about the system can manipulate it more freely than you might like. This suggests the avoidance of blind trust in one system wizard, together with enough safeguards to keep your data (if not the system itself) secure. Unfortunately, the class of systems of which we speak are frequently found in small firms that depend on one in-house person for all computer knowledge, and that makes the imposition of this level of security rather difficult.

Perhaps the most important part of this whole investigation into security is the simplest one of all: stay alert. Keep advised of all developments involving your system, and never let it become a mystery. The worst problems always occur in companies that see the computer as a mysterious black box that "somehow" produces data and prints checks. This is a situation ripe for abuse; indeed, it almost cries out for it. One employee with only scant knowledge of the machine can walk all over a company that is totally ignorant of it—and be gone long before the damage is discovered.

Know your purchase. This is the best security of all.

4.3 INSURANCE

Implementing every available security technique would, as we have noted, raise the operating costs of a system to an intolerable level. At some point, the impossibility of guarding against every possibility must be acknowledged, and the risk transferred to an outside agency. Fires, bombs, heavy vandalism, and those horrors called "acts of God" in legal contracts—all are capable of wiping out a computer room and even the most sophisticated of protective measures right along with it.

You probably wouldn't drive without car insurance, own a home without homeowner's insurance, operate a business without business insurance, or live without life insurance. It makes sense that you shouldn't compute without computing insurance. Unfortunately, it's a bit hard to find.

The problem is that still, after all these years, the staid insurance industry looks upon computers as somewhat mysterious and unquantifiable contraptions that represent an unknown risk. Even the prestigious Lloyd's of London, when queried about the subject over the phone, advised me to find a sympathetic broker.

Covering the system to the extent of its physical replacement cost is not difficult (as long as your other business insurance is with the same firm). Some agents may try to write the policy for the machine's "cash value" (replacement cost minus depreciation), but I don't recommend this: equipment becomes obsolete too quickly. Similarly, covering the magnetic medium for *its* replacement cost is no problem.

But the medium, in most systems, contains data. The data represent your business activity and may well have supplanted file drawers full of papers. A loss that destroys the medium takes with it the data, and this is where the problems arise.

A discussion with an agent of a "big-name" insurance company revealed the grim news: in their small-business owner's policy, valuable records are covered, except those in the form of magnetic media.

"You mean, if you can't see it, it's not real?" I asked.

He tried to reassure me by reading the next paragraph, emphasizing the first few words—which were, "magnetic media . . . are covered . . . ." Unfortunately, the last few words read, " . . . for the cost of the media in blank form."

In other words, a file can be insured if it is enclosed in manila, but not if it is enclosed in Mylar. The absurdity of this was pointed out to the agent, who verbally shrugged.

Finding a "sympathetic broker" is only the first step. You must also find a company with twentieth-century views on the world of computers, and the courage to extend traditional policies to new forms of media. Not all data on disk are unquantifiable: software packages can be purchased for known amounts of money, and data can be reentered or recovered from your off-site backup disks (you *do* have backups, don't you?) in a measurable amount of human time. But inevitably, some volatile information will be lost in a catastrophe, just as would be the case with traditional filing systems.

If you succeed in finding an enlightened insurance company, consider the various types of coverage that you might need. In addition to the machine itself and other physical manifestations of "the system," you may want accounts receivable, business interruptions, and extra expenses insurance. The latter is of use if your system is wiped out and you find it necessary to do business with a service bureau or to relocate your operation.

A bit of research revealed the encouraging news that some insurance companies are beginning to respond a bit more reasonably to these problems than the first few that I talked to. Perhaps by the time this is published, the behemoths will have come around.

One Minnesota-based firm, touted by a local agency as the leader in this field, indeed offers attractive "Mini-Computer" coverage. The option exists for replacement-cost valuation rather than cash value, and they cover data (based on your actual cost of reproducing them) up to a limit of $5000.

The usual catalog of restrictions applies, of course, with such problems as mechanical failure, fraud, verminous ravages, programming errors, strikes, and nuclear reaction left to you. Interestingly, any of these *can* be covered if a fire or explosion results: they won't pay for system damage caused by an atomic bomb unless the damage results from a *fire* caused by said bomb. It's a strange business.

The restrictions to the standard policy notwithstanding, the company goes so far as to offer an endorsement that will cover some otherwise uninsurable problems (the Breakdown Coverages Endorsement). With a $1000 deductible, they will cover losses incurred through faulty design, air-conditioning failure. equipment failure, or electric power surges occurring within 100 feet of the building containing the equipment.

So all is not lost. I present these two diametrically opposed views from different segments of the insurance industry to illustrate a vital point: don't just turn the problem over to your existing agent. Microsystems are far from rare now, but there is still considerable naiveté afoot in the land.

In any case, your insurance agent will probably insist that certain protective measures be taken to reduce risk to a manageable level. It's somewhat like the "safe driver" discounts: if your facility has good fire protection, decent security, and an enforced backup protocol, your rates will be lower. If they're not, shop elsewhere.

This whole subject of risk, which we are about to leave forever behind us, should never be far from your awareness. Even the casual system user with no need for secrecy can still suffer considerably if a disk is damaged. *At the very least,* even if you scorn fancy locks and high-priced insurance policies, make frequent backups and store them somewhere else. It's a nuisance and ties up some diskettes, but it is the cheapest insurance of all.

These past four chapters have focused on the system: its purchase, environment, maintenance, and destruction. Let us now make an assumption that will accompany us through the rest of the book: the machine is in place, it works, and it won't break.

5

The Human Environment

5.0 INTRODUCTION

Human readers of this book might justifiably be feeling a bit left out by this time, with all the emphasis on the comfort and coddling of machines. As you well know, implementation of a computer in any kind of working environment depends heavily on people, those who have to live with it and make it work. As obvious as this is, it is very commonly overlooked.

More than once, I have hung around in the shadows of a computer store and listened to the sales pitch. A businessman wanders in, asks about a system to do accounting and spread sheets, and finds himself regaled with tales of what various machines can and cannot do. Fine. He selects one.

But nowhere in the material provided by the vendor can be found information on actually integrating the wondrous contraption into his business. Can he just plop it down on the desk and have an instant "electronic office"? Or are there a few human considerations that need to be studied?

Clearly, the latter is the case. Human performance is every bit as important as system performance, but is more easily degraded by poor environmental conditions, demanding and unforgiving computer programs, and the belief that the machine is boss. In the next three chapters we will be considering ways of making the people as comfortable as the computers, as well as training, political and "territorial" problems, and such matters as user friendliness and software selection.

5.1 OPERATOR COMFORT

One of the unintended side effects of computerization is often the unremitting requirement of many hours of somebody's time at the helm of a CRT terminal. This is a crucial issue in employee acceptance of the system; if jobs that were once interesting are replaced by tedious data entry, people *will* complain.

But even without problems of tedium (which *can,* by the way, be avoided), certain environmental stresses are imposed by computer operation that should be taken into consideration. Many of these are already familiar. Constant noise, such as that from fans, disk drives, and printers, can wear on people's nerves after a while, and elevated temperatures can exacerbate human tempers, as well as stress the hardware.

But the real issue involves the many hours of interaction with a terminal that, before the computer, were probably spent dashing about the office interacting instead with everything from co-workers to copiers. It is not uncommon for an employee to arrive at the office, gulp the morning coffee, then spend the entire day in one position with hands poised over a keyboard. It becomes clear that some serious attention must be paid to seating, lighting, and terminal design, if employee health and well-being are to last.

For many years, little consideration was given to CRT terminal *ergonomics,* the study of the physical relationship between person and machine. Units were designed for the "average" user, whatever that is, and were often fitted with polished glass screens that caused glare. Keyboards were very different from those of typewriters, characters on the screen were blurry, and the physical characteristics of the units were unalterable. In short, operators had no choice but to adapt to the machines.

In time, the proliferation of computers (and operator health problems) began to turn the head of the National Institute of Occupational Safety and Health (NIOSH), which began a series of disturbing studies. Among other problems, it was revealed that full-time terminal operators were far more susceptible than other office workers to eyestrain, blurred vision, headache, back pain, numbness, and fatigue. Other studies highlighted the proliferation of serious eye problems, and at least one lawsuit occurred claiming that intensive CRT exposure had caused cataracts in employees.

With over 10 million terminals in use at this writing, and many more on the way, it has become clear that the old approach—making the user adapt to the machine—is no longer appropriate.

NIOSH recommendations are a good start. They suggest, first, mandatory 15-minute rest breaks after every two hours of continuous terminal use (or after one hour if the work load is intense).

Second, NIOSH suggests an ophthalmological examination at the beginning of employment and annual vision tests thereafter.

We will discuss the third item further in a moment: adjustable workstations that allow the operator to modify the seating arrangement, screen and keyboard height, and other viewing parameters.

Fourth, they encourage a general reduction of office lighting intensity, together with glare-controlling steps such as installation of drapes, screen hoods, and indirect lighting.

These matters are not trivial. For five years, I have done all my writing via the word-processing software of whatever system happens to occupy my office, and I can attest to the strain of extended periods at the keyboard. For some reason, it's a little worse than it was at the typewriter, perhaps because the discomfort is far less obvious and I tend to press on for longer stretches without respite. Fortunately, my latest machine uses a terminal that offers a low-glare screen with pleasant green phosphor, a separate keyboard, and adjustable viewing angle. Even the cursor can take one of five forms depending on my preference. Although it's a bit early to tell for sure (this unit is still pretty new), I am quickly becoming convinced that work is easier and more productive than it was with the ragged old thing that occupied center stage on my desk for the last few years. (Part of that increase in productivity can also be attributed to the use of friendly software, which will be discussed further in Chapter 7.)

The attention that should be paid to ergonomics in the selection of a terminal is largely a function of equipment cost and the intensity of the anticipated use. If the data-entry requirements are infrequent and/or money is a primary concern, it may be preferable to acquire the cheaper units that offer little in the way of flexibility. Most manufacturers sport a wide range of models.

But if the unit is to be in extended daily use, it would be well to relieve the operator of the need to assume awkward body positions in order to work. Everything should be adjustable: chair height, lighting, keyboard position, screen angle, footrests, intensity and contrast, position of reference documents, and even the loudness of the keystroke feedback (Figure 5-1).

While shopping around, look closely at the displayed characters on the screen. Do the lowercase letters *g*, *j*, *p*, *q*, and *y* have descenders? Those are much easier to read than the ones that are all crammed into the same horizontal stripe (or worse, are all captials), since the greater variety in letter shapes gives the brain more information in the form of visual cues.

Is there any perceptible screen flicker? This can be more easily observed by averting the gaze, since the retinal cells around the edges have evolved a higher frequency response to better alert the brain to peripheral motion.

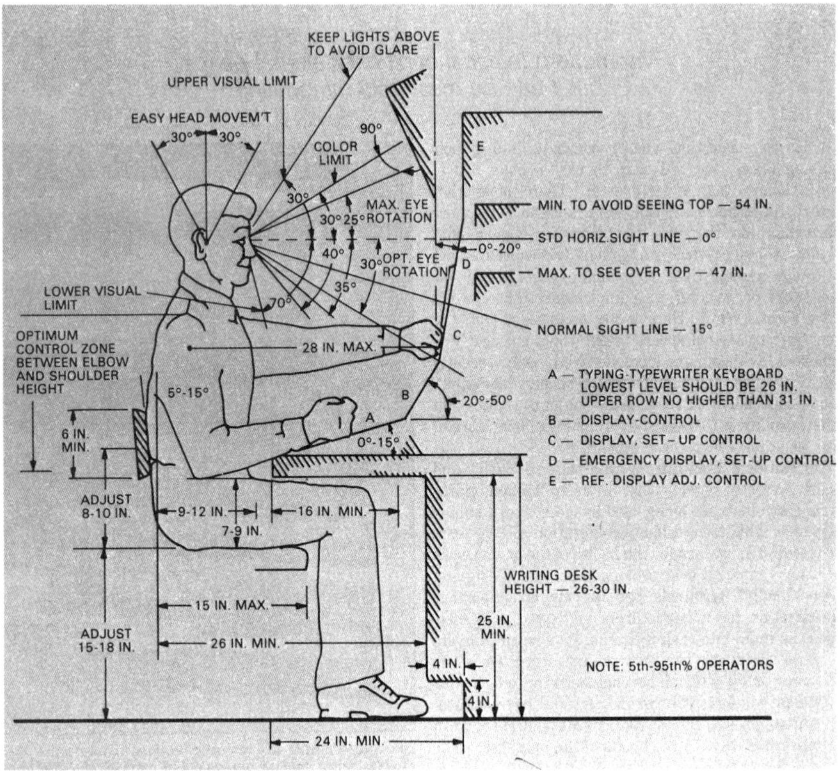

Figure 5-1 An ideal ergonomic workstation is one in which everything—from seating position to glare—can be optimized for maximum efficiency and comfort. (Chart is courtesy of Design West, Irvine, CA, and statistics are from *Measure of Man: Human Factors in Design* (published by Henry Dreyfuss & Associates.)

Flicker is caused by CRT phosphor of very short persistence, allowing it to return to black after each scan of the electron beam. But excessively long persistence can be annoying as well: it will cause streaks behind characters as they are scrolled upward.

Do the dots that form the characters blend well into lines—or at least look about the same horizontally as vertically? Some displays show bright horizontal lines wherever dots appear side by side, but distinct dots if they are vertically arranged. The effect is annoying.

Is the *aspect ratio* (the relationship of width and height) of the characters pleasing? Are the lines comfortably (and equally) spaced? Some problems of this nature can be fixed with minor display adjustment, but others are a function of the design.

Does the screen have a matte finish to reduce glare? If not, various polarizing materials can be purchased that reduce reflection while improving contrast.

Are similar characters clearly distinct from one another? *X* and *K; O, 0,* and *Q; S* and *5; I, 1,* and *l;* and *U* and *V* all frequently cause confusion. Although most applications will provide sufficient contextual information to make the distinction easy, this cannot be counted upon.

Is the cursor readily visible without being gaudy, and can it be easily found no matter what is displayed on the screen (including graphic characters and underlined text)?

Looking at other parts of the terminal, consider the case material. If it is textured and neutrally colored, it will resist dirt and fit into any office decor. It should not be glossy—the glare can drive operators to tape black paper over the offending surfaces.

Is the keyboard comfortable, with attractive keys and good spacing? Does it clatter or feel smooth? Is key depression ambiguous, or does it provide clear feedback in the form of beeps or clicks—and if the latter, are they sounds you could live with day after day? Is there a place to rest your hands? Is the numeric keypad organized in a useful fashion? Accountants are likely to view this question differently from those whose experience with numeric keyboards is most strongly associated with the telephone.

What about such features as graphics, editing capability, and programmable function keys? Although these are not ergonomic features in the truest sense, they have a lot to do with worker productivity and should be considered at the same time (Figure 5-2).

All these questions are designed to determine whether terminal use will be comfortable for hours and days on end. It is obviously difficult to make such a determination in the computer store, with a salesman's chin on your shoulder and an endless stream of features in your ear. The unit is new and fancy—of course it looks good.

The best way to get around this seduction is to find, accompanied by whomever will be spending the most time at the terminal, a unit of the same design in a low-pressure environment. Pour a cup of coffee, sit down, and type a long letter to an old friend.

Do you still like it, or have a few little things started to become annoying? This test is best performed with a system that has been in use for a while; the "new" will have worn off.

All this emphasis on the CRT, or course, is due to the fact that it is

Figure 5-2 The Corvus Concept personal computer offers numerous features geared toward operator comfort, including a low-glare multifont tiltable screen. (Courtesy of Corvus Systems, Inc.)

the primary point of interface between human and machine. But the same considerations apply, although less forcefully, to other system components. Printer noise, location of disk drives, and positioning of cabinets all affect operator comfort as well. You can assume that adjustments will be necessary as experience with the system is gained, and it is healthy to encourage frequent operator feedback concerning his or her likes and dislikes.

Before leaving the subject of operator comfort, we should touch for a moment on the computer room furniture itself. It is obvious that the seating arrangement should be comfortable, but you can carry the idea a lot further with a little effort. Try to anticipate normal work-flow paths, and arrange file drawers, work surfaces, and in/out baskets accordingly. Make sure that enough desk space is available for listings or documents being processed. Finally, check to be sure everything moves smoothly, including the swivel chair (if it is expected to roll on thick pile or shag carpet, it is not only an endless pain but invites static problems).

5.2 SAFETY

We have already touched on this subject a time or two, but it could stand a quick comment in the context of human considerations. Although these little machines are hardly threats to life and limb, a few cautions apply.

Shock, obviously, is a concern wherever electrical power is used. A well-designed machine should present no more threat than a typewriter, but it is possible to poke fingers into places that are hazardous. In particular, removal of machine covers with power on should be performed only by qualified personnel, since 115 volts—and in some places, much more—is present on exposed points.

More likely is back strain, which can come about not only from uncomfortable seating, but also from the conveyance of boxes of paper (averaging 40 pounds) from one place to another. Unfortunately, printers are often located such that it is necessary to lean over them to change the paper supply, and this can place considerable strain on the operator's lower back.

In our discussion of computer room design, we also mentioned the need to keep power cords and cables under control. Small systems are often carried about more like appliances than business equipment, and the wires connecting the various units are commonly left to fall where they may. People can trip.

In general, safety problems are no more severe than they would be in an old-fashioned, noncomputerized office. Common sense is your best guide.

5.3 PSYCHOLOGICAL CONSIDERATIONS

We come now to an issue that has some very serious ramifications. Comfort is necessary, but even the most ergonomically optimized system in the world can cause employee unrest, job dissatisfaction, ennui, and rapid turnover. It is probably safe to observe that people problems are at the root of most computerization failures.

5.3.1 Employee Problems

The most obvious class of these problems can be generally characterized as employee resistance. For a variety of reasons, employees can be distressed by the introduction of office automation, despite demonstrable increases in efficiency and productivity.

Although it may, in a sense, be true that office automation relieves people of certain repetitive tasks and frees them to make decisions and handle problems outside the computer's capabilities, the reality is often a degradation of working conditions. A CRT terminal displaying one data-entry form after another is just as demanding as an assembly machine in a factory, using a human to perform tasks that happen to be impossible for the computer. In many office environments, the employees have simply become machines that enter data into other machines.

Such a situation might well be *efficient* in terms of throughput, but it threatens the very foundation of the business: its people. I have frequently heard comments about boredom, wasted skills, assembly-line conditions, and loss of motivation. Indeed, the typical approach to office automation redirects the once-diverse activities of individual employees to repetitive tasks performed at the console of an inhuman "boss." Absenteeism increases, attitudes fall apart, and the desire to excel falls away in the face of limited opportunities for advancement beyond certain levels.

Added to all this is an underlying fear of computers that somehow persists after all these years. The shroud of mystery that has surrounded "thinking machines" since their inception is still very much in evidence.

In the old days, it was reasonable to think of computers as great, mysterious machines occupying special air-conditioned buildings and waited on by a scurrying staff of white-jacketed technicians and myopic computer scientists. Even though these lumbering and inefficient leviathans of yesteryear possessed but a fraction of the capabilities found in today's average desktop system, they *were* awfully big, and certainly foreign to the experience of most people. The mystique was largely attributable to the popular media, which breathlessly gushed stories about thinking machines the size of the Empire State Building that would someday outperform the human brain, and huge computers humming away underground somewhere in Washington that know something about each of us.

Films showed computers exploding into flames when asked the Ultimate Question, small-time politicians looking for the Big Image stood before spinning reels of tape during TV commercials ("I have just directed this computer to *cut your taxes!*"), and financial institutions began hiding behind the inscrutable facades of IBM systems that could obviously do no wrong. Now that they outnumber us, is it any wonder that people find it somewhat difficult to relate to computers?

I've had a home computer since 1974, and still, some random visitor will occasionally gaze wide-eyed at my little system and say, "Can I ask it something?" or "Have you got anything in there on me?" It is easy to chuckle at this naiveté, but it becomes a serious problem when you announce to your long-established office staff that the new machine being unpacked is going to computerize their jobs and make them more efficient. The average employee will feel like an accessory to the machine, rather than the opposite.

It is obviously worthwhile to dispel the negative notions and work very carefully to involve office workers in the decision-making processes associated with the new system. A computer can be a wondrous tool, but if it is allowed to define the shape of the work to which it is applied, the roles reverse and people become the tools instead.

There are a few specific recommendations that can reduce the probability of this occurrence.

First, as we have already suggested a time or two herein, employees who will be working with the computer should be involved in its selection, and in the myriad decisions related to its implementation in your business. Rather than inflict a new method of handling accounts, for example, solicit suggestions on how it should best be done. It may well be that their ideas (which are firmly rooted in daily experience) will result in even greater increases in efficiency. In any case, the message you send them is clear: you care about their opinions, and they have some control over how the mysterious new machine will be used.

Second, always strive to cater first to the people, not to the computer. The assembly-line conditions can be avoided, partially through selection of friendly software and partially through attention to the environmental factors discussed in the first part of this chapter. Software packages that call the shots and use the human operator as nothing more than a barely adequate data-entry machine do not lead to job satisfaction.

Third, avail yourself of every opportunity to dispel the fear and mystery surrounding computers. Computerphobia is not pleasant, and it can even be seen in some operators of point-of-sale terminals, who treat every transaction as if it were a test of their competence and intelligence. In Chapter 6 we will spend some time on a gentle introduction to the whole subject that can be used in an employee education program to demystify computers somewhat. Anyone can be "trained," rodentlike, to perform a series of arbitrary steps, but if they are educated instead, those steps will make perfect sense. This allows easy handling of exceptions and changes without confusion, and gives the person an otherwise-absent feeling of confidence and mastery over the machine.

Fourth, many long-time employees will resist the need to change work habits and abandon systems that have worked for years. Many, in fact, will maintain completely parallel manual systems for quite some time after computer installation, trusting only data that appear on index cards and ledger sheets. The best way to deal with this problem is to make the new procedures philosophically equivalent to the old. The flow of information through the system thus makes sense in the light of experience, even if the exact details are a little fuzzy. The key to this is, again, education: if the employee understands that a file on disk is analogous to a file in the battered old cabinet across the room, it is a little easier to trust the machine with information that was once handled manually.

These recommendations may call for a change of course in the implementation of the electronic office, especially since most computer vendors tend to downplay the difficulties. Ads for systems emphasize performance, quality, features, reliabilty, and support, but seldom do they address questions of employee resistance. How could they? That's the *user's* problem.

5.3.2 Executive and Territorial Problems

We wouldn't suggest, of course, that such difficulties are limited to employees. Although managers at various levels are probably isolated somewhat from the moment-to-moment drudgery of data entry, they are every bit as susceptible to computerphobia and the "old dog" syndrome.

Interestingly, one of the biggest problems is that a lot of executives either hate to type, can't, or don't want to be caught at it. Yet when an "executive workstation" hosting a typewriterlike keyboard appears on their desks, they are suddenly confronted with a task that they perceive to be rather secretarial in nature. They've spent perhaps 25 years in company management and are not only suspicious or afraid of automation, but simply unwilling to learn the "menial" skills necessary to cope with it. The underlying reason may be stubbornness, ego, or fear, but the net effect is a marked resistance to change. (Figure 5-3)

The irony of this is that most executives spend 20 to 30% of their time on low-productivity tasks such as scheduling and chasing about for information. With 77% of the roughly $600 billion annually spent on office wages going to executives and managers, it is clear that substantial savings could be had if office automation were to be adopted across the board. But for the reasons outlined above, most of the change has been centered in the clerical arena, perhaps because the personnel involved don't have the power to resist change as successfully as those who call the shots.

Solving the problems of executive resistance begins with the same points made earlier, but may, oddly enough, call for even "friendlier" systems to overcome that fear of doing secretarial work.(Figure 5-4) In addition, you can introduce new facilities on a pilot basis and involve those affected in a decision-making role.

Some of the problems will simply solve themselves: it is not uncommon for peer pressure and fear of obsolescence to outweigh computerphobia. But

Figure 5-3 (Copyright 1982, Universal Press Syndicate. Reprinted with permission. All rights reserved.)

this still doesn't take care of a situation that often develops in companies that are large enough to be departmentalized: territorial disputes. Data-processing folk may claim the office automation facilities as part of their domain, since the technology involved is congruent with their own. Administrators stake out territory in the computerization arena because the facilities cut across other departmental boundaries. Word-processing or office-management types out their familiarity with the people and the work flow. Engineering people nod knowingly at the hardware and mention something about technical support.

Another problem is the actual shift in the balance of power within a company. There have been many cases in which a firm installed a complex computerized information system to streamline financial reporting and work flow. But in the process of accomplishing those objectives, it gave substantially more information to corporate-level management while decreasing the control of lower-level and divisional people. This had the effect of generating hostility between the information bosses and the rest of the work force. Motivation in the lower levels declined as they felt less influence on the company as a whole, and gradually became aware of decreased upward

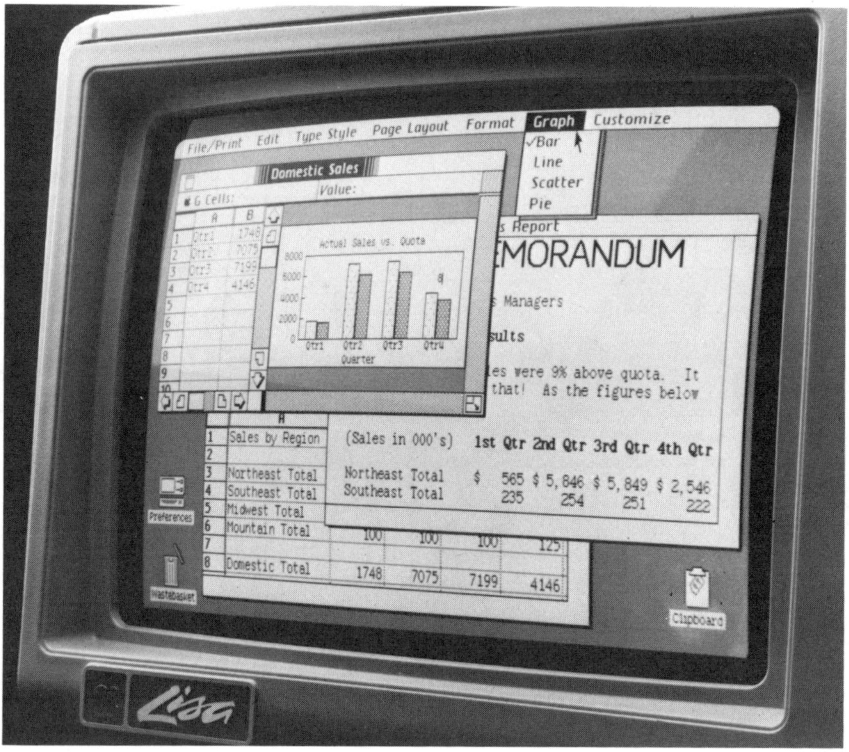

Figure 5-4 The Apple Lisa Computer can all but eliminate dependence on a keyboard, except for actual data or text entry. The screen can display up to four applications simultaneously, with functions selected via an easy-to-use "mouse" pointing device. (Courtesy of Apple Computer, Inc.)

mobility because of the "information gap" generated by the shift in balance of power.

It is possible in such a setting to undermine the social benefits of worker cooperation, leaving a coldly efficient structure in which individuals are highly specialized nodes in a computer-controlled hierarchy. The traditional friendly interdependency of office workers gives way to employee resistance against the new, dehumanizing structure.

When implementing a system, it is wise to anticipate some changes in worker relationships and to provide ample education to reduce the inevitable impact. Further, the needs of the people (upon whom any business ultimately depends) must be taken into account before an optimally efficient system is inflicted on the organization. Some of the costs are not immediately obvious.

All this is of little concern, obviously, in the *very* small business. If you run the whole show, questions of territories and worker hierarchies are absurd. But if not, it is worthwhile to draw on the expertise of all departments (to avoid overloading any one) and perhaps create a new position of "information manager" to oversee the entire operation.

We seem to stray somewhat from our avowed orientation to the world of microsystems. That would be the case but for the fact that micros, these days, are not necessarily thought of as insular, task-dedicated machines. Local networks tie diverse processors together and allow electronic mail, paperless exchange of files, sharing of the more expensive resources, and an atmosphere of integrated information processing. But to all of these applications, people are still the key.

Since we determined that education about the system is a central issue in the smooth implementation of same, let's spend a chapter on the methods by which the learning process can be simplified. I constantly see small business owners, keen on the idea of acquiring a system, sign up at the local university or technical school for a night course in BASIC or COBOL programming. They are driven to this by the shortage of general introductory information and by the belief that learning to write programs is essential to the smooth installation of a computer.

It's not. Let's see what *is*.

6

Demystifying the Computer

6.0 INTRODUCTION

As mentioned in Chapter 5, many of the "people problems" can be prevented before the fact by simply making sure that the machine is not a mystery. An employee who has always held a responsible position in your operation is liable to look askance at a mysterious contraption called a computer that is going to "improve efficiency." Worker displacement is a hot issue.

And what about you? It's obvious that *you're* not going to be replaced, but is your conception of the system clear? Do you understand what occurs when you run a program, or are you just accepting the vendor's claims on faith and hoping that it will somehow do what he says? Are the sequences of commands that must be typed somewhat arbitrary, or do they make intuitive sense?

The answers to these questions should tell you something. If the computer is a mysterious black box, no amount of program documentation can take away the uneasiness that accompanies conversion of your old reliable information-handling methods into electronic form (especially after reading the cautions and horror stories in the first few chapters of this book!). Some computer education is in order.

Before you skip ahead with the conviction that this chapter is full of obscure jargon, binary calculations, and arcane concepts, let's talk about your car.

Unless you are a mechanic, you probably don't know the precise details of cam timing, carburetion, automatic transmission hydraulics, and suspension damping. You probably don't really care. I don't, anyway.

But you *do,* I'm sure, have a basic working knowledge of what's going on in there. You can probably name and give a brief functional description of most of the entubated modules cluttering the engine compartment, and when a little red light comes on that says, "ALT," you very likely know that something in the battery-charging circuit has gone over the hill.

This level of knowledge about a car is adequate for the average driver. Only if you wish to become a mechanic or an automotive hobbyist does it become worthwhile to dig into the details. When you have occasion to drive, the sequence of controlling operations makes perfect intuitive sense, and you probably don't have the disquieting feeling that your life is depending on some form of magic.

When we talk about computers, however, a rather different effect occurs. Unless you are a "computer mechanic" or hobbyist, you probably haven't the foggiest notion of what's going on in there, even though your perusal of this book suggests that you are about to enter into a rather dependent relationship with one of the little beasts. Does it make you a little uncomfortable? Would it, if your life depended on reliable operation?

Computers, actually, are incredibly simple. They certainly are less complex than color television sets, and contrary to popular opinion, they don't involve much math. They are complete idiots that can only do one thing: follow a sequence of trivial instructions. Of course, they can do this with considerable speed, and it is this, not any intrinsic complexity, that enables such wondrous tasks as data base management and word processing.

This chapter is devoted to a jargon-free overview of computers. If you're an old-time data-processing wizard or microprocessor hobbyist, you can just skim it and move on to some of the techniques, but if you are new to the game, I strongly recommend taking the time to read this closely. I also recommend considering it as the basis of an employee education program that will make subsequent system-specific training a lot easier for all concerned.

6.1 THE HARDWARE

We will be considering the computer system in two parts: the hardware and the software. The former can be described as that collection of tangible items that take up space in your office and carry a manufacturer's logo on the front panel; the latter consists of sequences of instructions that tell the hardware how to do something useful.

The hardware components that make up your system may vary, but all installations will have a few things in common. In particular, you can be sure that somewhere in your system is a *central processing unit* (CPU), so let's begin with that.

6.1.1 The CPU and Memory

The general objective of any computer is the manipulation of data. This can take many forms: the handling of text (as was the case during the writing of this book), the generation of "spread sheets" such as expense reports and pro formas, the processing of payroll, the calculation of flight information in space shuttles, the control of an industrial machine, bibliographic search through a system-resident library of references, and the simulation of battles with aliens in an arcade game. This wide diversity of applications implies the primary feature of computers: they are general-purpose machines. In the old days, tasks such as those outlined above could be performed (if at all) only with specialized and dedicated hardware. This was not very cost-effective.

Various people had the idea of building a machine that could perform a variety of basic functions, then *programming* its operation through the use of punched cards or tape. These primitive contraptions enjoyed varying degrees of success, gradually evolving into the monstrous computing systems that occupied whole floors of buildings and gave rise to all the mystique. In time, of course, the machines were compressed into some reasonable spaces through the application of solid-state electronics (transistors, then integrated circuits), and they became affordable to organizations other than big business and government.

But what, exactly, is at the *heart* of these general-purpose machines?

Take a long look at Figure 6-1, for it is the model we will use throughout this entire discussion. Showing everything but the CPU, the drawing includes a wall of numbered "post office boxes" (the memory), a couple of file cabinets (the disk drives), and some windows to the outside world (the terminal, the printer, the modem, etc.). Everything but the CPU. For purposes of this discussion, we will cast *you* in the role of the CPU.

All this isn't as whimsical as it sounds. From a philosophical standpoint, we can totally ignore all the details of interconnection—all those cables, parts, and connectors you see when you pop the top off your system. A computer can be very neatly defined as a set of independent facilities such as those shown in the figure.

One thing must be firmly clarified, however. Although we will be

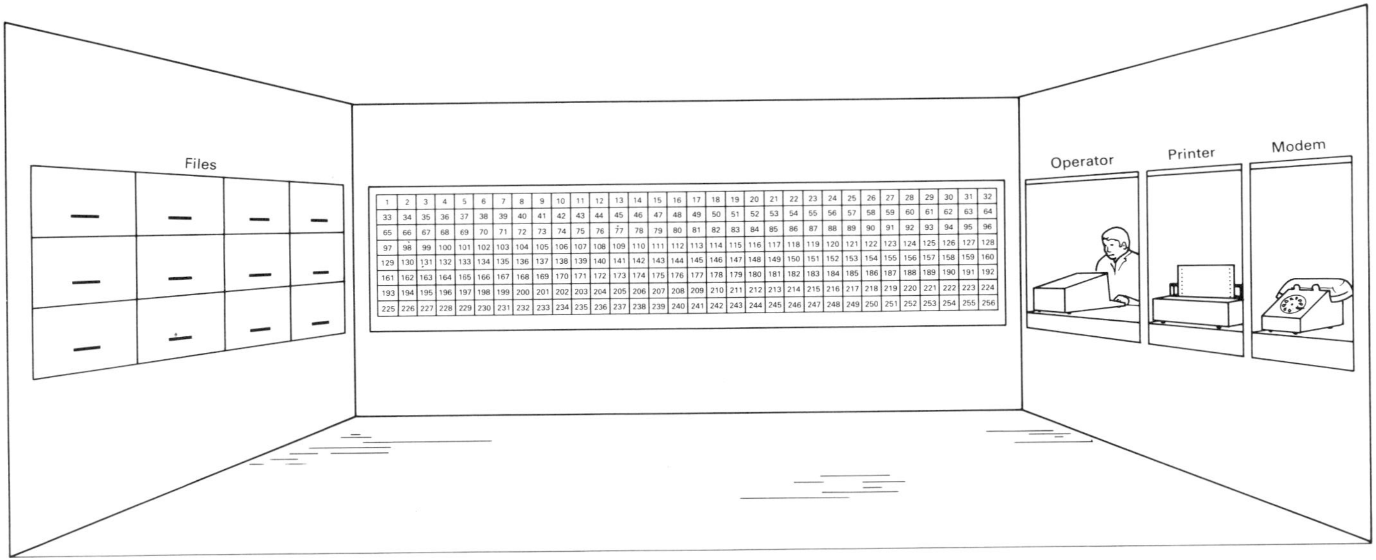

Figure 6-1 This somewhat whimsical model suggests the computer from the CPU's point of view: the memory is the wall of post office boxes, the disk drives the file cabinets, and the I/O devices are "windows" as shown.

casting the CPU into the second person to make it easy to identify with, we would hardly suggest that there is any similarity between a sentient human and a processor. The CPU has no intelligence, no "self." It is an uninspired piece of hardware that, while quick and accurate, is as dumb as (nay, dumber than) your pocket calculator. Our analogy will quickly fall apart if you think of the CPU as anything like the imaginary human that is walking around in there.

OK, what *is* it like? Consider the requirements. Its basic task is the performance of a sequence of instructions in order to do various things to data—move them from one place to another, modify them, and make "decisions" on the basis of them in order to alter the system's default path through the instructions. These requirements pretty well govern the technology, and all the different processor designs stem from variations in detail, specifications, and architectural philosophy. Those needn't concern us here.

Given a piece of hardware that somehow provides this "instruction execution" capability, we can begin to see how it interacts with the facilities sketched in Figure 6-1. Please put on your CPU hat.

As a central processing unit, you possess a few basic capabilities. These have nothing to do with any particular application, or even with any language. (It is common for people to ask, upon viewing a computer, "what language does it use?" The correct answer is *none*—languages are programs just like everything else. But we're skipping ahead.)

Somewhere on your back is a RESET pushbutton (I know this is a bit corny, but bear with me). Someone pushes it, and without appreciable delay, you stride purposefully over to the wall of post office boxes and remove a slip of paper from box 1. There is an "instruction" written on it that says, $B = 5$. You poke through the dozen or so little notepads in your pockets, remove the one prominently labeled *B*, and write the number 5 on it. You have no idea why.

Once this is complete, there is only one thing to do. Leaving the $B = 5$ instruction in box 1, you open box 2 and find another one very much like it: $C = 200$. You locate a notepad labeled *C*, and write the number 200 on it.

Moving right along, you find a different kind of instruction in box 3: $A = (C)$. You happen to know that this means, "write on notepad *A* the contents of the box whose number is written on *C*." So you do just that—you look at *C*, note that it says 200, then walk over to box 200 and extract a small piece of paper. On it is the single letter *h*. You write that on your notepad labeled *A*. At this point, you have three pieces of information: $A =$ "*h*", $B = 5$, and $C = 200$.

Even though the last box you "addressed" was 200, that was not an instruction; it was data. So you return to the next one in sequence, box 4, which says, *OUT CRT*. Since you were designed to respond to such an instruction by handing a copy of whatever is on notepad *A* to the CRT terminal, you walk to the "operator" window, write the letter *h* on a little slip of paper, and hand it over (whereupon hardware separate from the computer briskly causes it to appear on the terminal screen).

That done, you move to box 5. The instruction is: $C = C + 1$, or, "add 1 to the value written on notepad *C*." You do that, leaving the number 201.

Box 6 contains a similar command: $B = B - 1$. You dutifully subtract 1 from the number on pad B, leaving 4.

The next one is a little more interesting. The instruction reads, *JUMP IF NOT ZERO TO BOX 3*. This refers to a *flag* called ZERO, which will be "on" if the result of the last calculation was 0. Since it wasn't, ZERO is inactive, and your instruction execution has just been transferred back to box 3, where you pick a character from the box whose number is written on notepad *C*.

Of course, *C* is now 201, not 200, so instead of the *h* you found last time, you find an *e*. Going through the "loop," you dutifully pass that to the terminal, add 1 to *C* (yielding 202), subtract 1 from *B* (yielding 3), and check again to see if the ZERO flag became active. It didn't.

You do it again, finding the letter *l* in box 202. Then again, finding another *l* in box 203. And then yet again, finding an *o* in box 204. You have just written "hello" on the CRT terminal.

At this point, you are still following instructions. You come for the fifth time to box 6, whereupon you subtract 1 from the number written on notepad *B* and discover that the result is zero. You activate your ZERO flag.

On your fifth execution of the *conditional jump* in box 7, something different takes place. Instead of jumping back to 3 as you have been doing, you simply fall through to box 8, since ZERO is inactive, the condition of the jump instruction is not met.

So, eager to be doing something else for a change, you extract the contents of box 8: *HALT*. You have no choice but to enter a state of suspended animation (or computation?) until some *deus ex machina* intervenes to again press your RESET button. (Figure 6-2)

As trivial as this whole example may seem, we have managed to hit most of the high points of computer operation. The CPU spends all of its time either following simple instructions or waiting in the HALT state.

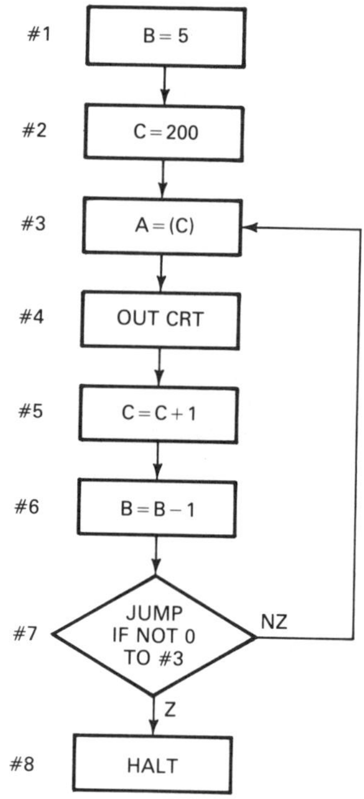

Figure 6-2 Flowchart of "hello" program demonstrates the steps described in the text. The word "hello" is stored in memory starting at location 200.

Instruction execution proceeds sequentially through memory from the lowest location, unless directed otherwise by some kind of instruction. The CPU only "knows" what's written on its little notepads (registers), and it is capable of moving data only one chunk (character) at a time among its registers, memory locations, and input or output devices.

Obviously, there's quite a conceptual leap that needs to be made between this primitive device and a working system. The key is buried in that sequence of instructions—for without it, the computer is inert. Before progressing, however, let's take a moment to relate the scenario sketched so far to reality.

The wall of numbered post office boxes, of course, is the system memory (not to be confused with disk drives, which we will discuss shortly). It generally takes the form of a few integrated circuits—fewer and fewer as time goes on and circuit density increases—that are closely wedded to the CPU itself. In many cases, they share the same circuit board. Should you happen to peer inside your system, you would probably find some multiple of eight identical chips all in a row, connected by numerous parallel "traces" on the circuit board. The odds are good that they comprise the memory.

Much of the revolution associated with the microcomputer field is attributable to the compression of the CPU into one chip. Even though the operations we characterized above are philosophically trivial, it is clear that the need exists for hardware that can keep track of data, somehow interpret the instruction codes found in memory, perform simple arithmetic, and communicate with input and output devices. Fortunately, that is all done for us by the microprocessor, rendering the overall design of the hardware substantially less complex than it once needed to be (Figure 6-3).

Incidentally, the absurdity of the term "electronic brain" should start to become obvious at about this point. Computers, at least at their present level of development, are pathetically restricted by the information bottleneck implied by the need for all instructions and data to pass sequentially through a single CPU. Even in multiprocessing environments, where numerous computers work together on a multifaceted task, each one is but an incarnation of the post office paradigm: a CPU fetches one datum at a time from memory, then trundles off with it to turn some primitive logical crank.

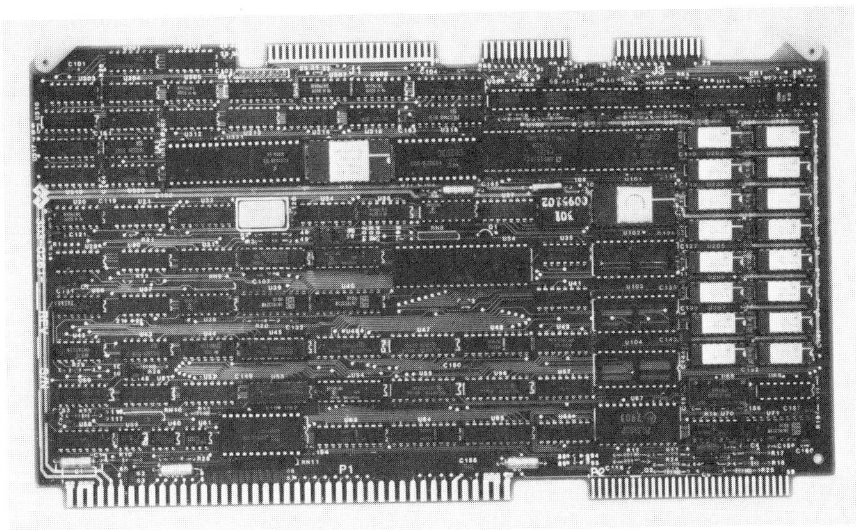

Figure 6-3 A typical robust computer-on-a-board is the MSC-8009 from Monolithic Systems. This industrial-grade unit is the heart of the author's word-processing system, and includes 64K of RAM, a floppy disk controller, two serial communications ports, a Z-80 CPU, a timer, some ROM, and an interface to the bus to accommodate expansion. (Courtesy of Monolithic Systems Corporation.)

It is safe to anticipate future departures from this approach, but the technology is nontrivial.

A further appreciation of this may be gleaned from a comparison between your brain and any computer you care to consider. Even though the machine may be touted as a powerful processor capable of executing millions of instructions per second, it pales in comparison to the biological system. This is interesting because individual neurons in the brain take thousands of times longer to react than do the logic elements in the computer.

The staggering performance difference is attributable to the fact that in the brain, there is no part that can be called a CPU. Millions of widely dispersed "processors" work together on a task, rendering something like recognition of a face or understanding a newspaper article so easy that you seldom have occasion to marvel at the accomplishment. But for a computer to do either of these things, it must operate on one tiny datum at a time—a single dot of the facial image, for example—and then somehow integrate all the calculations into some kind of useful result.

There are areas, of course, in which the computer quite outshines its human masters. Any task involving logical operations on sequential information (text, business accounts, industrial control measurements, etc.) can be performed more quickly and accurately with a computer. But as soon as some level of global or holistic understanding is required, the machine begins to look pretty pitiful.

Anyway, for our purposes, this limitation is acceptable. We're not asking the machine to run the business, just take over some of the tedium. Let's continue with our scenario.

6.1.2 Inputs and Outputs

All computer applications depend, at one point or another, on communication between the machine and the outside world. All the processing horsepower in existence is of no use if it is ensconced in a sealed black box, forever *incommunicado*.

In our foregoing example, the CPU executed a short program that resulted in the appearance of the word "hello" on the CRT terminal. We saw that it was accomplished by handing the message, one character at a time, through a "window" in one of the system's "walls."

The truth is that input and output (I/O) devices are seen by the computer very much as memory locations. "Reading" the keyboard of the terminal, for example, is accomplished in the same basic way as reading the contents of one of those post office boxes.

Let's relate this a little more to actual experience. When you sit down at a terminal and begin typing, the system must have some way of inhaling that information in an organized fashion. If it was just frantically reading the keyboard over and over, it would probably see a "t" as "tttttttttttttt," for the CPU is so much faster than your finger that even a quick stroke of the key lasts quite long enough for multiple passes through that part of the program.

Of course, the computer would read nothing at all if it were not in the process of executing a program that tells it to look at the keyboard—to walk over to that window, see if there is a piece of data, and take it if so. It has no initiative, nor is it psychic. You can bang on a keyboard all day long, and if the CPU is performing some other part of the program, you will be ignored.

Typically, the circuitry inside a terminal responds to the depression of a key by converting it into the appropriate character code (that "h" in our earlier example is 01101000—but there should never be any occasion to worry about such things), and then sending it to the computer. Circuitry in the computer (at the window, not in the CPU) then holds that code and *sets a flag* indicating that a character has been received and is being held for pickup.

There things stay, possibly forever, unless the CPU is directed by appropriate instruction to check the keyboard "window" for an available character. That flag (just a yes/no condition) is itself testable by the system, and when the CPU discovers that it is active, it can jump to an appropriate part of the program where, presumably, it is directed to read the key itself. The process of reading the key then clears the flag and makes another one possible.

This type of activity occurs every time you strike a key (if the system works, of course). If you are not typing, and the system is just sitting there waiting for a command, then the CPU is spinning endlessly in a loop: "Did anybody hit a key yet? No? Well, did anybody hit a key yet? No? Did anybody hit a key yet?" and so on. It's a tedious life.

When somebody finally *does* hit a key, the CPU grabs the data as described, then does whatever is appropriate to the program that is running. It may add the data to a command that is being pieced together for subsequent comparison to a list of commands (such as TYPE, RUN, PAYROLL, BASIC, and so on), or it may just add it to a block of text being created in memory that will soon be printed as a business letter. The key may be a backspace, which is nothing special except that, because of the program, it usually causes the previous character typed to be erased. It could be anything, and it could be interpreted in any fashion. It is *entirely* up to the program.

The range of possible I/O devices is probably unlimited. Terminals and printers, of course, are the most common, but in various environments you will find maps, pushbuttons, machine control circuitry, graphics displays, speech synthesizers, robot arms, motors, traffic lights, missle guidance systems, and almost any imaginable kind of sensor. Every single one of them is grafted onto its "host" computer system with circuitry that makes it compatible with its I/O design. Depending on the type of computer you have, you may find that you can purchase "I/O cards" or "adapter cards" for exactly this purpose.

6.1.3 Disk Drives

As you probably know, disk drives are a mighty important part of a small system. As suggested by Figure 6-1, they are the file cabinets which house essentially all programs and data (I say "essentially" because a few central programs, such as the one that tells the machine how to come to life, are stored in devices called *read-only memories* in the computer itself). All applications software—accounting, word processing, whatever—is acquired in the form of disks, and as your operation progresses, you build a library of files containing business records, text, and so on. All on disk.

The CPU knows nothing about disks, but it can follow a sequence of instructions to interact with them. Basically, all it needs to do is move information from disk to memory (that's where the little slips of paper for the "hello" program came from), or vice versa.

Needless to say, the program that makes this possible is rather elaborate, and fortunately, there is seldom any need for a system user to think much about its operation. In Section 6.2.1 we will discuss the organization of data on disk and something of its handling; for now, let's content ourselves with a look at the hardware.

Disk drives are essentially I/O devices, but their crucial role in a system justifies special treatment. Charged with the task of maintaining all the machine's information in some kind of organized and error-free fashion, they are perhaps the most critical of all system components. Being mechanical, they are subject to wear and tear, and as we noted in the maintenance chapter, a large percentage of system problems can be traced to them. Actually, they are a major pain—but necessary.

A typical floppy disk drive is dedicated to the task of rotating a piece of magnetic medium (very much like a thick, round piece of audio tape) at a constant speed, then positioning a *head* accurately enough to read or write data on one of many concentric circular *tracks*. That's the whole point of a disk drive.

In practice, it's not quite that simple. Speed is of the essence, so various competing schemes exist to move the head back and forth, and data integrity is critical, requiring very careful design. The disk drives are connected via cables to a part of the computer known as the disk controller, and respond to commands from the processor in a fashion that brings about the desired data transfer. This involves the manipulation of *files,* which in one way or another embody all the information of interest to the system user.

It becomes obvious here that a lot of trivia has to go on in order for the disk drives to do their job. What if you erase a file, then try to replace it with a bigger one? This is certainly necessary, but it requires quite a bit of effort on the part of the program, and this is why *disk operating systems* are such a big deal in the industry. It would be completely unacceptable if you, the user, had to be aware of the details of disk operation; indeed, this was probably the greatest single impediment to the early acceptance of small computers in business environments. As we shall see shortly, the "system" as you see it is not a CPU–memory–I/O–disk conglomerate at all; it is a carefully designed program which simply organizes all of *your* programs. Bear with me, this will make sense by the end of the chapter.

6.1.4 The Terminal

When the "hello" program delivered five successive characters through the appropriate I/O channel to the terminal, it had no need to give much "thought" to the means by which they appeared graphically on the screen. It would be worthwhile for us to discuss this a bit, not because you should ever have occasion to think of the terminal as anything more than a "black box," but because there seem to be some widely held misconceptions concerning the meaning of what's on the screen.

The terminal, although in the context of our earlier discussion is a window into the CPU, is capable of communicating only one character at a time. (This is not the case if your terminal is described as a "memory-mapped" unit.) That fact can be a bit misleading because it is sometimes tempting to view *the entire screen* as a window into the system.

The actual operation that takes place when a character is transmitted to the terminal is its conversion into an appropriate graphic form (that 01101000 for "h" would be a bit confusing) and its subsequent display on the screen at the present cursor position. Clever programs (such as WordStar, VisiCalc, and others) manipulate the cursor to give the illusion of a full-size window into the system. This, of course, is possible only with terminals that are "smart" enough to respond to cursor-control commands.

In the simplest case, a terminal simply accepts characters one by one and puts them on the screen, with the old material *scrolling* upward as new lines are added. Clearly, this old material is not guaranteed to reflect the current status of the system, a fact that is sure to cause confusion to some beginning operators. (Old-style text editors, for example, depended on a "virtual pointer" to some location in the text, which was in no way discernible from the appearance of the screen.)

Modern terminals exhibit varying degrees of "smartness," which allow all sorts of extensions to this basic display of characters (Figure 6-4). Of particular interest in applications characterized by the filling in of "forms" are the units that provide "foreground/background" capability and protection. These allow the system to identify invariant text on the screen by presenting it with dim or reversed characters, making it easy for the operator to visually separate the variable information from the form itself. Other features include local editing (where a screenful of text can be manipulated before it is sent to the computer), but with most system designs, all this is quite handily

Figure 6-4 The Televideo 950 CRT terminal represents one of the early affordable units with a separate keyboard, as well as a healthy variety of display options under microprocessor control. (Courtesy of Televideo Systems, Inc.)

accomplished by the system itself. Some programs do, however, take good advantage of the editing features to eliminate the need to rewrite the whole screen when something is changed.

Fortunately, the terminal can usually be considered a functional unit by the user, with the only interconnection required taking the form of a single cable. This interface is called *RS-232* and is widely accepted as a standard, making different terminals more or less interchangeable.

6.1.5 The Printer

Printers, like terminals, interact with the computer through a communications channel that is one character wide. Normally, this information transfer is unidirectional (except for timing information on the order of, "Hold it, I'm busy "), with characters appearing on the paper more or less as they were received—after spending some time in a buffer to allow the mechanics to catch up with the electronics.

Various styles of printers have appeared to address different market requirements. Most common in the small-system world are *matrix printers* (Figure 6-5), which form letters and numbers on the paper by striking it with appropriate "dots" as a head moves across the page. The head consists of a vertical line of usually seven or nine wires, any or all of which can be rapidly driven toward the paper to make an impression through a ribbon. Internal circuitry in the printer, not entirely unlike that in the CRT terminal, converts the character codes from the computer into the appropriate combinations of dots that will result in readable text.

Matrix printers are generally fast and inexpensive, since the number of moving parts is held to a minimum. The only problem with them is that characters formed of dots are not universally considered to be of "corre-

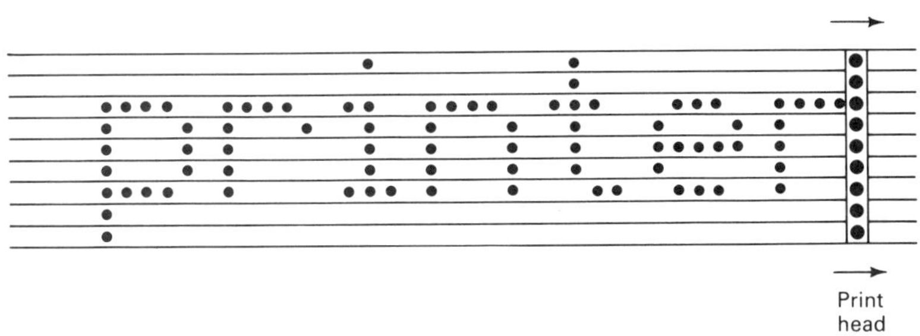

Figure 6-5 Matrix printers (of the classic variety) are based on a print head with a column of solenoid-driven wires. This is swept across the page as the wires are "banged" appropriately, yielding text or graphics.

spondence quality." A number of techniques can be applied in the printer design to approach the fully formed characters comparable to those of office typewriters, but a discerning eye can still distinguish even the best matrix print from that of traditional machines.

Presumably, the widespread use of small systems and affordable printers will eventually eliminate this bias in favor of fully formed text, but in the meantime, the problem can be very neatly solved by the other major contender for your printer dollars: daisy wheels. Marketed by Qume, Diablo, NEC, C. Itoh, and many others, daisy-wheel printers have become the standard in word-processing applications because of their extremely high print quality. They are notably slower, less flexible, and more expensive than their matrix cousins, but are generally considered to be well worth the difference.

In a daisy-wheel printer (Figure 6-6), a head moves across the page, carrying with it a circular printing element that bears 88 or 96 individual tines. At the end of each tine is a raised character which, when positioned appropriately and struck from behind by a small hammer, makes an impression on the page via either a fabric or carbon film ribbon. The speed of such units ranges from 30 to 60 characters per second (compared to well

Figure 6-6 Daisy-wheel or "letter-quality" printers depend on a print wheel such as this one, which is rotated to the proper position and then struck with a hammer. They are thus slower than matrix types, but almost faultless in print quality. (Courtesy of Uarco, Incorporated, 121 North Ninth Street, Dekalb, IL 60115.)

over 100 in many matrix printers), but the difference in type quality is considerable.

Like terminals, printers can usually be considered "black boxes" from the user's standpoint. This is just as well. Let's move on to a quick overview of a few other kinds of I/O devices, then consider the real issue: software.

6.1.6 Other I/O Devices

As mentioned earlier, there is hardly any limit to the range of I/O devices possible. Your application may require nothing beyond those already described, or it may call for custom interfaces to production machinery or data collection equipment. This section is provided to sketch a few other common peripherals and suggest some of the possiblities implied by the computer's generality.

Possibly the most common accessory beyond the basic system is a modem (for *mo*dulator/*dem*odulator), which interconnects your system with the telephone line. There are more and more reasons every day for you to have this capability. In my own installation, I use the modem for at least three types of activity: information retrieval and research through the SDC Orbit and Lockheed DIALOG systems, exchange of information with my associates via electronic mail, and transmission of manuscripts directly to the publisher's compositor. My last book, in fact, passed from my diskettes to a large DEC system in Washington, D.C., whereupon it was edited to conform to Prentice-Hall's manufacturing specifications and then typeset. At no point was it necessary for anyone to sit down at a keyboard and reenter all of my carefully proofread material, taking extra time and introducing errors.

More and more services are coming into existence that are of general interest to the business and professional system user. Various vendors provide a wealth of information online, which can be exhaustively searched to yield business trends, patent abstracts, bibliographic references, legal information, medical news, and a wealth of specialized material. Considering the fact that you already have about 85% of an on-line terminal in the form of your CRT, adding a modem to make it useful in this context is a relatively minor expense.

The modem, in its simplest installation, replaces your computer as the entity on the other end of your terminal's data cable. Converting the "bit stream" of characters into sound and doing exactly the opposite to received information, the unit allows access to any dial-up computer service.

A more sophisticated communications option involves the addition of another I/O channel to your computer, a minor task that has been made even easier by plug-in modems such as those made by D. C. Hayes (Figure 6-7). These simply plug into your system, taking care of the I/O logic and the modem circuitry with one simple addition. If this approach is taken, you are not limited strictly to "terminal" applications; you can transfer files from your computer to another and back again.

Other optional I/O devices include alternative methods of human–machine communication, such as speech synthesiers and recognizers. What was once formidable is now becoming quite straightforward (at least in limited applications), with speech-generating boards available from a number of suppliers. Converting text to speech is not too difficult, but going the other way is still plagued by problems. Essentially, it is impossible to separate human language from intelligence (although perusal of certain tabloids might lead one to doubt this), and any system charged with the task of truly recognizing speech must be able to extract the differences of meaning

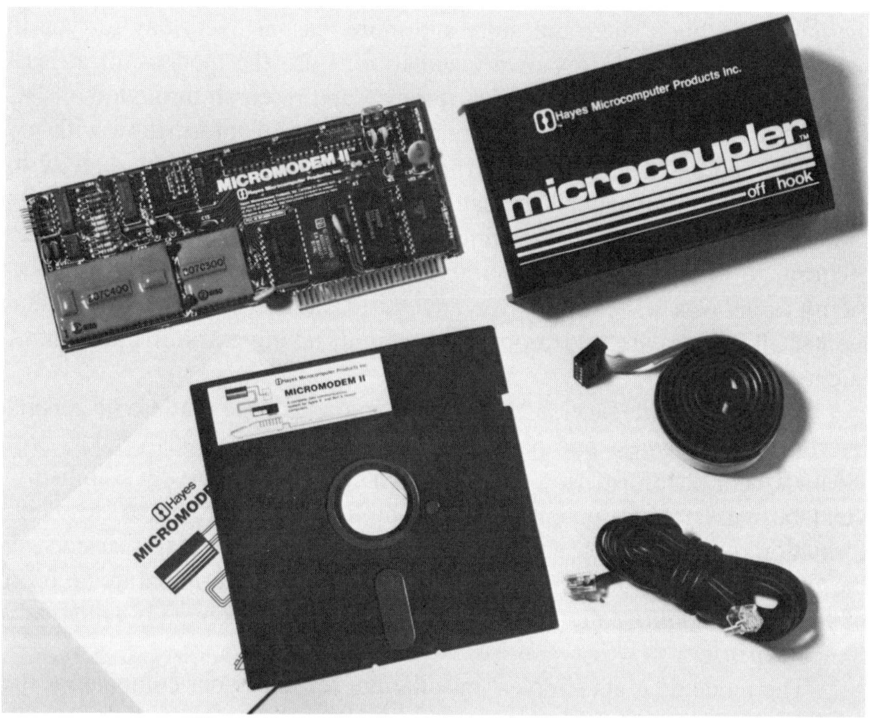

Figure 6-7. A popular accessory for the Apple (with versions available for other computers) is this direct-connect modem from Hayes. This approach eliminates the need for classically unreliable acoustic couplers, and can be entirely software controlled. (Courtesy of Hayes Microcomputer Products, Inc.)

buried in context. This problem is serious enough that commercial applications of speech recognition are still limited to small-vocabulary tasks with experienced users.

All sorts of other I/O devices are possible, ranging from complete systems in the next office down the hall to a little red light at your desk that flashes when someone makes an error. It is easy to add a "real-time clock" for those applications that would be served by knowledge of the time (such as an appointment or security system), and communications lines to remote points can be tacked on with no more difficulty than a modem. The generality implied by the computer's fundamental design extends to the environment in which it works, so it is probably safe to observe that just about any kind of contraption can be grafted onto it—assuming that you are willing to pay someone to design the interface.

With that, let's move on to the essence of this whole industry: software.

6.2 SOFTWARE

As we have had occasion to observe a time or two, the computer is not worthy of much consideration without some software. It would be like celebrating a turntable without any records.

Software is the point of the computer business, and it should be your primary concern when you are buying a system. The most sophisticated engineering in the world is of no value if it yields a machine that is unsupported by competent programming effort—another reason to be wary of "specsmanship" when shopping around.

A number of interesting issues have arisen in the software business over the years. Since the real cost of any system design is becoming weighted more and more heavily toward human time, it has become worthwhile to begin speaking of programmer productivity and software standards. These very practical considerations are not always well received by the independent renegades that make up a fair share of the world's programmer population, for much of the traditional excitement in writing a program has always involved cleverness and trickery. Imposing management objectives on such a business is bound to yield some discontent.

Rampant wizardry hardly seems like a bad thing. After all, some rather spectacular software has arisen from wild-eyed denizens of the world's computer rooms, and it seems sad and a little unfair that the industry is making a swing toward standardization.

But the rationale is clear. Programmer time is almost prohibitively expensive, and the effort involved in fine-tuning an obscure masterpiece might price a software product out of the market—or delay it so much that the question of pricing is moot. In addition, it can be assumed that the original programmer of a system will not always be around to fix errors or make modifications, and baroque code, albeit poetic, may be only so much randomness to the person saddled with an update task. More than one custom system has faded into obscurity in just this fashion.

For these reasons, techniques have achieved prominence that bear such monikers as "structured design" and "portable code." The former implies a "top-down" approach to a task, comparable to the design of a corporate hierarchy; the latter implies the avoidance of machine-specific code that would forever marry a design to the system on which it was developed.

If you should happen to become involved with a custom software project, you should be aware of some of these issues. As we discussed quite a bit earlier in the book, you can become quickly orphaned if you become dependent on a completely unique program . . . however brilliant it may be. Sad, but true.

Let's look now at the "principles of software"—first with an eye toward insulating ourselves from the gritty details of the computer, and then with the intent of teaching it to do something useful.

6.2.1 Layers of Code

According to Section 6.1.1, life at the CPU level is not very pleasant. Despite the elegance and generality implied by the scenario of Figure 6-1, actually dealing with the system at the "machine" level is so grim that real business applications would be impossibly remote. How can you address questions of inventory control and patient data base management when you can feel the bits between your toes?

It is to this end that the standard resources known as "operating systems" exist. Somebody painstakingly writes a program that puts the CPU through all the paces necessary to print a file from disk, requiring only that the user tell it which file it should print. When you sit down at a terminal and enter the command "TYPE HELP.TXT" a considerable amount of work is going on below your awareness as text begins spewing forth.

Operating systems differ widely in detail, with some supporting multiple users, others optimized for fast file manipulation, and still others reflecting the biases of their designers or the characteristics of the CPUs that host them. It would be of little value for us to explore these differences, but a look at the basic principles might save you a lot of later confusion.

The overall purpose of an operating system, no matter what anyone else tells you, is the establishment of an insulating cushion between you and your machine. It is weakly analogous to the control panel of a photocopier, which provides three basic controls: number of copies, darkness, and START. If you had to put the copier through its paces step by step, it would be much easier to just retype the document.

The operating system will provide you with a small group of *intrinsic* commands: features that are built-in, essential capabilities. Typically, these will allow you to do such things as call forth a file directory, erase a file, display it on the screen, rename it, and so on. But before we go any further, what's a file?

In a cabinet to my right are a hundred or so manuscript files. In a 3 × 5 index beside the terminal is a deck of cards (yeah, this will all be on the computer someday, but who has the time?) that comprise a *directory* to the files themselves. If I want to pull a file corresponding to this book, I look in the alphabetized directory, find that the manuscript number is 71, then open the big drawer and remove that file folder. I find that folder by reading its label—its filename: MS-71.

None of this is particularly esoteric. It is of interest, however, because it is remarkably similar to what goes on in a computer when I type "DIR" on the terminal to look at a file directory, choose the one I want, then request that the system type it. The software of the operating system accepts the filename that I type on the terminal, then scans through its drawers to find one whose name matches. If none do, it says something like, "File not found." If one does, it "pulls" the file and makes it available.

If I want to erase the file, all the system has to do is wipe out the label. Even though the information is still out there on disk somewhere, it has been cut off from access by the removal of its name—and subsequent storage operations will write over the space that the data once resided in.

The key to all this is the directory, which must obviously be a little more than a simple list of names. If it is displayed on the terminal, all I see are the names, but associated with each one internally is information concerning the locations on disk that are occupied with the file, its "status" (which tells the system whether it is okay to write over it or erase it), and its size. Clearly, destruction of the directory is tantamount to destruction of the disk.

The files themselves can consist of just about anything imaginable. In our example, it was convenient to think of text, but it could just as easily have been financial data, employee records, or a program.

This last possiblity raises an interesting question: How does the system distinguish between different kinds of files? At the CPU level, of course, it doesn't. If you direct the system to read a text file from the disk and display it on the terminal, it does just that, with no understanding of what's going on. But if you want to *run a program,* you want a file to be seen differently. The computer must be told that the file consists of a sequence of instructions that need to be loaded into memory (the post office boxes) and performed. It is an operation akin to pulling a file folder out of the cabinet, opening it to discover a stack of paper slips inside, and distributing them one by one, in order, throughout the boxes beginning with some predetermined location.

There's nothing to stop you from doing this with a text file, either, but if you then direct the system to execute it, you will find the results to be garbage. Similarly, displaying a "machine-level" program on the terminal yields gibberish.

For this reason, many operating systems include some built-in protection against this kind of error. "Command files," or those that are designed to be loaded into memory and performed by the computer, are designated (in the CP/M operating system) with the suffix ".COM". Attempting to run a file labeled "GARBAGE.TXT" then simply creates an error message.

For the moment, this distinction of program and text will suffice, but there must, of course, be a way to print programs in a way that makes sense to human beings (or else there would be no sane programmers). We'll get to that in the next section.

Anyway, the net effect of all this business with files and directories introduces a welcome isolation between the human being and the computer. Long ago, those who interacted with computers had to know most of the details of the hardware design in order to work effectively. Now, with this cushioning blanket of code called an operating system, it really doesn't matter *what* kind of computer is in there, as long as files are manipulated in a useful and repeatable fashion.

From the end user's standpoint, this is fine: if it is ever necessary to dig beneath those cushioning layers, it will be too soon.

But *somebody* has to program the beast. Somebody has to convert an idea into that explicitly coded form that will cause the CPU to carry it out. The process would be an incredible pain were it not for programming languages.

6.2.2 Languages

The term "language" is actually a little bit misleading, conjuring images of computers sitting around chatting in French. To establish agreement on the meaning of the term, let's start with the human communication process.

When one person sets about to say something to another, some very interesting phenomena take place. The speaker has in mind an idea, something nonverbal and relatively abstract. Perhaps, given the intended focus of this discussion, we can consider the idea to be a task that the speaker wants the listener to perform: say, emptying the wastebasket.

Now this is hardly a difficult concept, but consider what takes place as the speaker and listener interact. First, you (the speaker) conjure an internal image of the task. The wastebasket, presumably, is full, so you visualize it empty and associate a certain employee with the operation necessary to make it so. As the employee stands before you awaiting instructions, you begin *mapping* that abstract visualization onto a more tangible, verbal level (try it). This process is subconscious but is carefully tailored to the relationship that exists between you and the person you are addressing (Figure 6-8).

This is the key. Assuming for the moment that you could get away with asking anybody in the world to empty your wastebasket (don't try it), think about the different levels of communication that would take place. Depending on the prior relationship you had with the person, the instructions would range from the very explicit ("Please take this trash can out the door, down the hall, through the second door on the right, and out to the green dumpster in the parking lot, then empty it and bring it back") to the cryptic

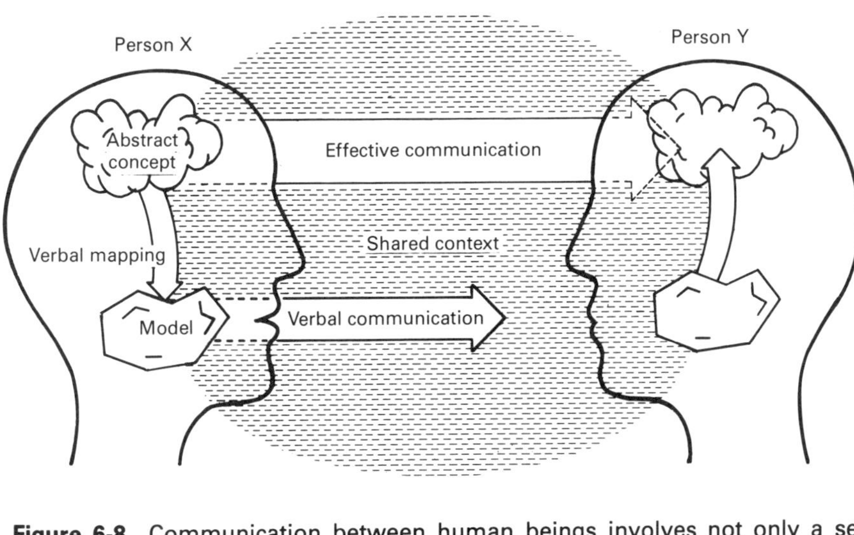

Figure 6-8 Communication between human beings involves not only a sequence of words, but also an extensive shared context. The net effect is a substantially higher degree of efficiency in the communication process than would be the case if everything had to be stated explicitly. (From Steven K. Roberts, *Creative Design with Microcomputers,* © 1982, from page 158. Reprinted by permission of Prentice-Hall, Inc., Englewood Cliffs, NJ.)

("This is full"). The difference depends not so much on the intelligence of the listener as on the *shared context* that exists between you.

For the cryptic instruction to make any sense, you and the employee must share certain key aspects of your knowledge about the world. The employee must know what *this* is, what is implied by the fact that it is full, what needs to be done, and how to go about doing it. Your speech is "automatically" adjusted to a level that suits the degree of shared context present between you and the listener.

As the verbal utterances pass through the ether from your mouth to the employee's ears, a complementary phenomenon takes place in the other brain. The words, together with appropriate contextual information, are linked together and used to project the verbal model upward into abstract conceptual space—yielding, if you have communicated successfully, a notion comparable to the one in your head that started the whole affair. "Ah, it's full indeed. I'll take care of it." Or at least a surly "yeah." In any case, you have probably not had to trouble yourself with details.

Now. What's all this got to do with computer programming? Suppose, for the sake of argument, that your company has just taken delivery on a new Cybertronics utility robot, but the vendor's harried sales department forgot to send any software. Sitting in your office is an inert contraption with wheels, arms, and a computer just like the one we wandered around in following instructions on slips of paper. The mechanical parts of the robot, we can assume, are appropriately interconnected with the computer's I/O ports such that proper combinations of command codes can put the machine through its paces. You decide to make *it* empty the trash. All you need to do is write a program (Figure 6-9).

You have a problem. There is no shared context: the machine doesn't even know what a trash can *is,* much less what to do with it when it is full. "Explicit" instructions involving references to doors, hallways, and dumpsters mean nothing to it. You know exactly what you want the machine to do, but it is going to take a few months of dedicated programming effort to tell it exactly how.

Presumably, some software arrives while you are pondering this awesome task (and coming to the realization that just making the robot go through a door without crashing into the wall is a rather sticky problem). You heave a sign of relief, slip the disk into the drive, and load up the robot's command *language*. Depending on how well it is written, you can now identify the location of the trash can, specify its dimensions, and give the order to pick it up with some assurance that this will actually take place.

But you still have to perform some rather extensive elaboration of your verbal model ("please take this trash can out the door, et cetera") to yield

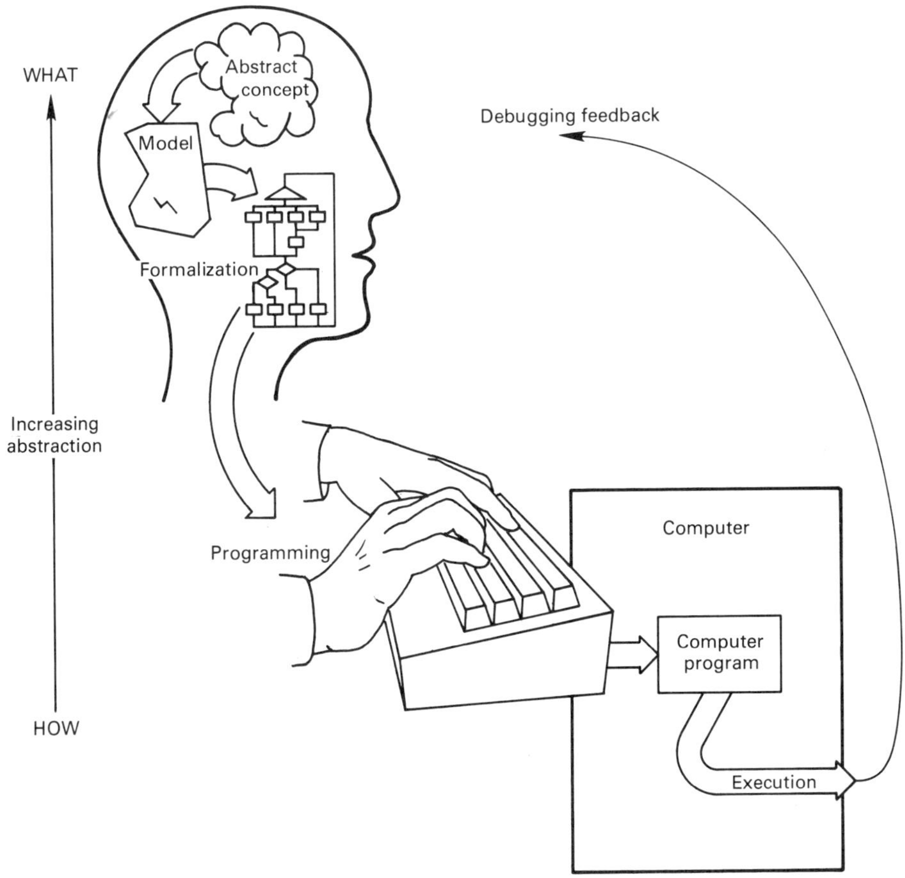

Figure 6-9 Replacing "person Y" of Figure 6-8 with a computer places a much greater burden on "person X," for he must now carry the verbal modeling process much further—producing an explicit, unambiguous description of the original abstract concept. (From Steven K. Roberts, *Creative Design with Microcomputers,* © 1982, from page 160. Reprinted by permission of Prentice-Hall, Inc., Englewood Cliffs, NJ.)

a program that will cause the robot to carry out your orders. You *still* have to tell it "how" although not quite so explicitly.

It is easy to imagine successively higher levels of robot language that would eventually enable you to give the same kind of verbal order you gave your employee. But the problem is obvious: as languages reach a higher level, they become inseparable from intelligence. This whole issue gives rise to an image of computer languages as points along a "what–how" spectrum (Figure 6-10): at the "what" end is the natural human language that embodies rich shared context; at the "how" end is the machine code that takes the form of detailed little instructions in post office boxes.

So where does that leave the computer business? At the moment, we're not too far removed from the "how" end, for even though some wondrously sophisticated software tools exist to facilitate the conversion of an idea from its intellectual form to its coded form, someone still has to issue step-by-step instructions with no assumption of a shared context. At this level, the robot trash program would be performed identically if you handed the machine an armadillo and sent it after a mythical dumpster on a deserted beach. No intelligence. It would just empty the armadillo and bring it back to you.

So when someone, inevitably, walks into your office and gapes at the new computer, then asks "what language does it use?" as if seeking to establish its alma mater, just mumble something about armadillos and hand him this book.

Before we leave this entertaining subject to return to more immediately practical matters, it is necessary to establish one more component of *our* shared context that will enable me to write the word "language" without being misunderstood. A language is just a program that accepts another program as input, then produces lower-level code as output. Let's take that a little more gently.

Since the ultimate objective of a program is the conversion of an idea from its "what" to its "how" level, it is clear that a programming language, as we have described it, is nothing but a tool that helps to accomplish this feat. Even though much of the work is still up to the human being, the

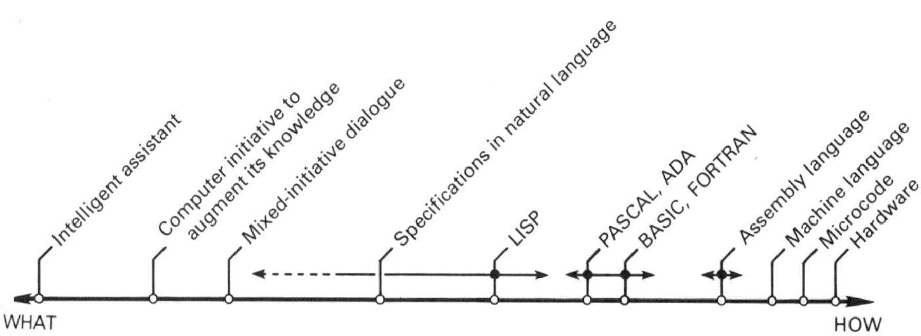

Figure 6-10 The what–how spectrum illustrates the range in levels of expression necessary to communicate with a system. (From Steven K. Roberts, *Creative Design with Microcomputers,* © 1982, from page 162. Reprinted by permission of Prentice-Hall, Inc., Englewood Cliffs, NJ.)

language eliminates that ever-grittier downward plunge into the depths of machine-level code. Merely a program itself, it accepts as its input a text file containing the high-level code, bites off a line at a time, and produces an output at a lower level. In the case of the common language BASIC, for example, the command *A = 4*LOG(X)* may result in hundreds of post-office-box-level instructions. The BASIC statement is thus much closer to the "what" level than the code that the machine sees, and it is converted when the program that includes it is *compiled* or *interpreted*.

Thus, there is really no such thing as a "native language" in a general-purpose computer, although some new systems are being designed to lend themselves more readily to one than another. The system here can quite briskly switch from BASIC to LISP to PL/I to COBOL—and as long as I am careful to give each one the right kind of *source code,* I can take advantage of the features of each as the application dictates.

That's right. Different languages are useful for different things. Further encumbering the robot analogy, we might find that the language suitable for emptying the trash can is not too good for assembly-line precision welding, and changing the baby's diaper might require a third set of language features. So we buy three languages: JANITOR, FACTORY, and NANNY.

6.2.3 Applications Software

Now we have two different kinds of insulation that can help maintain a comfortable distance between us and our machines. Operating systems allow manipulation of the system's resources (files and I/O devices) without the need for an understanding of how they are all structured, and languages permit us to devise programs at a level that is not entirely alien to human thought. Presumably, all this leads up to something: What are we going to use it for?

It would obviously be absurd to attempt a characterization of all possible computer applications in anything approaching a specific fashion. But perhaps we can preface the upcoming chapter on software issues with a comment that ties our foregoing discussion into the world of the end user.

A well-designed software package will complete the isolation between user and machine that was begun by the operating system and the language (Figure 6-11). In some "turnkey" systems, so named because turning a key is supposedly all that is necessary to fire them up, the operator never even has access to the operating system. Files are automatically loaded and executed upon power-up, rendering the machine no longer a general-purpose computer at all: it becomes a word processor, an accounting system, or whatever.

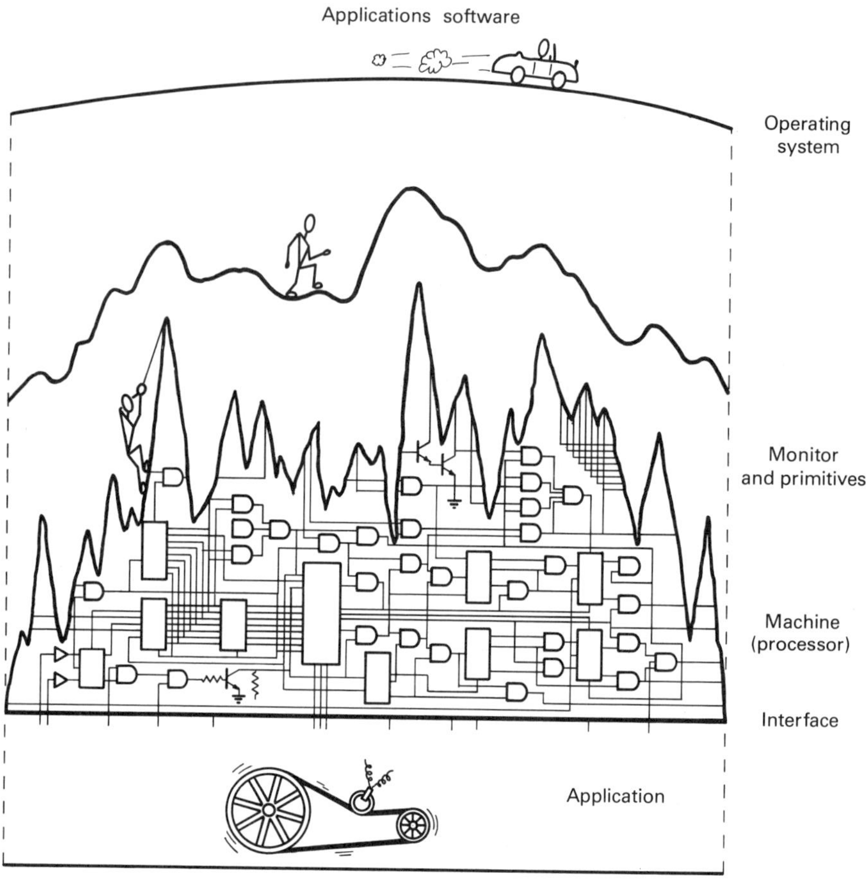

Figure 6-11 Much of the purpose for operating systems, languages, and applications software involves the cloaking of the craggy and forbidding machine-level "terrain" with insulating layers that smooth the programming task for human beings. Many levels of code may lie between the application program and the application itself. (From Steven K. Roberts, *Creative Design with Microcomputers,* © 1982, from page 173. Reprinted by permission of Prentice-Hall, Inc., Englewood Cliffs, NJ.)

There is a tradeoff to be considered here. When you buy a computer, you are buying, more than anything else, generality. One of the neat things about computers is that they let people get away from the hardware specialization that characterized machines of old (remember posting machines, card sorters, and Justowriters?). It would be a shame to wrap the computer so thoroughly in an application-specific cloak that it can never emerge and move on to other matters, wouldn't it? A good application software package will provide the user with the illusion of specificity without a permanent loss of generality.

Most other applications-related issues are so closely allied with the details of the task that we would sacrifice our own generality by addressing them. Let's go ahead and spend a chapter on some of the more pervasive software matters, and then move into some of the actual mechanics of keeping the system running smoothly.

7

Issues in Software

7.0 INTRODUCTION

The point of this whole technology—of processors and their peripherals, of operating systems, of maintenance contracts and vendor relationships—is the dependable performance of programs that do something useful. Now that we have discussed much of the surrounding technology, we can turn our attention for a while to some of the considerations that should be kept in mind when selecting, using, or writing software.

7.1 SOFTWARE SELECTION

The first step in selecting appropriate software from the thousands of packages that populate the burgeoning market has, we hope, already been accomplished. That is the establishment, in unambiguous terms, of exactly what you want your computer to do for you. It isn't enough to say, "handle the paperwork" or even, "track inventory" if you haven't developed a clear image of your information-processing requirements.

This doesn't require computer expertise, although an early understanding of what a machine can and cannot do will help separate dreams from reasonable objectives. But even lacking that, it is necessary up front to break your information-handling tasks into specific steps and then spell out in detail what, exactly, you want your computer to do. How much information has to be accessible at any given time? How many people will need to use the machine? Will it be necessary for more than one person to do so at a time? What kind of output do you need: letter-quality print, matrix print, graphics, or something special? What are the tasks that the machine must perform, and to what extent do they share the same body of data?

The answers to questions such as these, combined with the feelings of the people who already do the work that you anticipate handing off to the computer, will start to give you a practical feeling for the software requirements. As you learn more and more about the capabilities and limitations of computers, these ideas will begin to coalesce into a definable specification.

It becomes obvious very quickly that it makes sense to select the software before the hardware. You will very likely find that only a relatively small subset of the world's available software is just right for your application, and it would certainly be a shame to discover that none of it runs on the computer you bought. This happens with depressing frequency. Only a few days ago, a friend traded in his one-month-old machine for a different model after discovering to his dismay that the only available programs for it were inappropriate. His problem could have been avoided by choosing the software first, then finding out what kind of machine would adequately host it.

We keep warning about the danger in not learning a computer's limitations, and perhaps it makes sense to provide a few guidelines.

A computer won't solve all your problems, save money by eliminating workers, clean up errors in your manual procedures, revitalize your business, magically strengthen your market position, operate infallibly, or think. These things come as a shock to some people, thanks to science fiction that is all too often purveyed in advertising as fact.

With the exception of a very small number of systems that are in the research stage, computers are not very good at anything requiring judgment. They can do a pro forma, for example, but not a job estimate requiring insight and knowledge of your business. It may be possible to define all the steps in a task that traditionally depends on human judgment, and then computerize *them,* but anything further implies intelligence (although not necessarily human).

Machine intelligence is a provocative subject, guaranteed to elicit a wide range of reactions from people of varying sociological and theological persuasions. Although it seems unlikely that computers will soon possess anything as ineffable as *consciousness,* it is not only likely but already a *fait accompli* that they will exhibit intelligent behavior. At the moment, this takes place through the rather laborious modeling of human cognitive processes on hardware that is about as poorly suited to the task as it could be. But even with this intellectual strait jacket, systems have been developed that can exhibit startlingly intelligent behavior within sufficiently limited domains.

The hardware limitation to which I alluded is that funneling of all activity through a single processing site, as we discussed in Chapter 6. It is very safe to assume that upcoming hardware generations will be less distinguished by their speed or miniaturization than by their increasing similarity to the brain's hierarchical structure.

We are not really wandering off into esoterica with this discussion. In the context of traditional "business applications," talk of *machines who think* seems to be idle musing. Intelligent billing machines? If they were intelligent, wouldn't they find something more interesting to do?

But consider the evolution that is taking place in office systems—and what is really implied by the term "paperless office." Networking of multiple computers has become commonplace, increasingly sophisticated tasks are being relegated to machines, and talk of user friendliness has become almost a cliché in the business. When you consider that some of the tasks we might like to share with machines involve understanding of context (even at the word-processing level—consider spelling correction), and that friendly interfaces require enough intelligence to at least simulate understanding of human wishes, it becomes clear that artificial intelligence in the office isn't ridiculous at all. It will be nice to emerge from the dark ages.

Anyway, selection of software begins with the gradual alignment of your expectations with the available reality. Armed with a technologically feasible specification, you can then do a quick check for cost justification and begin casting about for a software package (unless, of course, you discover that the cost *isn't* justified after all).

Where? Where does this "casting about" take place? A good start is the plethora of small-system magazines that come and go as the industry grows. Spend a few hours in a well-stocked bookstore and find the ones that seem to be most aligned with your priorities. They change their focus regularly, so I won't document a characterization of individual publications, but you are sure to find two or three that are reasonably well suited to your application. Read the ads as well as the editorial material, and follow up everything of interest with direct inquiry.

Another printed source of information is books, but they have a habit of staying the same while technology progresses. The exceptions are those that avoid specific product references (like this one), but they aren't much help in choosing between a a pair of directly competing software packages.

Explore as many different computer stores as you can. Track down satisfied users and try out their systems. Do the same with unsatisfied users.

After a while, a few leaders will probably emerge. Most system applications fall within a relatively small number of major categories, and these are well recognized by the software vendors. You are thus likely to find many competing products in the areas of word processing, sorting, mailing-list handling, spread-sheet preparation, accounting, time management, data base manipulation, and so forth.

At this point, the scope of your problem changes. You must now make a selection from among many superficially similar programs. This calls for the juggling of a few trade-offs: capability versus memory requirements, innovation versus the advantages of a "standard," flexibility versus simplicity, and the usual cost/performance ratio. In addition, it is necessary to consider *all* aspects of your purchase at once, since two different and equally necessary programs may require mutually exclusive system resources.

Most of the other purchasing considerations are equivalent to those we explored in Chapter 1, involving such matters as customization and vendor support. So instead of belaboring those points, let's look into some of the other software issues that may have a bearing on your system.

7.2 USER FRIENDLINESS

In the early days of computers, few people were concerned about the ease with which nonspecialists could operate the machine. Computers were *supposed* to be obscure; this strengthened not only the egos of those involved with them but also their job security. I have even been guilty of that myself: there was a perverse pleasure, back in the good old days, in watching a visitor marvel at blinking lights and fingers flying over the 40 or so switches on the front panel of my first homemade system.

The trouble with all that, from the standpoint of the computer business, is that it doesn't take long to saturate a market made up of people who can relate to the innards of a machine. Microprocessors and their associated technologies would not be nearly as pervasive as they are if they were useful only to engineers and hobbyists.

Of course, system manufacturers have been claiming for years that their systems are "turnkey" and easy for even the beginner to use effectively. There was a time when any claim of that nature was pure nonsense.

Things are changing. Future writers of books like this will probably make similar charges about the 1980s, doubtless with considerable justification. But the fact is that it is becoming possible for nontechnical folks to interact smoothly with a computer (such as Apple's Lisa) without first having to learn machine-language programming, details of the system architecture, and the various forms of arcane notation necessary to decode the operator's manual.

Ideally, we would like to have computer systems that fit so smoothly into an application context that their presence is accepted as easily as that of a new employee. We would simply teach it the details of the task, assuming all the while that it has enough common knowledge that explicit, step-by-step explanations are unnecessary.

We're not there yet, but systems *are* beginning to appear that incorporate some features designed to further soften the insulation between human being and machine that we discussed in Chapter 6. This suggests a gradual departure from a procedural approach to computer operation in favor of one characterized by the manipulation of *objects,* just as you would manipulate paper files, letters, and notes. The first well-supported system with this kind of capability was the Xerox STAR, and in 1983 the Lisa appeared to bring such capability into the office at something approaching a reasonable price.

The objective is the establishment of a style of human–machine interaction that is closer to driving a car or playing a video game than is the traditional method of typing commands at a terminal. The latter offers no visual feedback beyond the appearance of the typed characters; the former provide continuously changing information that enables the operator to make fine adjustments and more accurately approach whatever goal is involved. You wouldn't want to control an automobile with a CRT terminal, since funneling such a dymanic activity through a restrictive command-oriented communication channel would probably be fatal.

Another problem connected with this is the handling of operator errors. Forcing someone to enter counterintuitive commands into a machine is bad enough without creating confusion with such useless messages as "SYNTAX ERROR." Just this morning, I received a call from a new small system user who was receiving that message consistently while trying to make a BASIC program work. The problem was simple; he wasn't putting quotation marks around a piece of text that he wanted the program to print. But why couldn't the machine tell him that? Instead of pointing to the error and explaining what was wrong, the computer just scolded him with "SYNTAX ERROR" and then sat there inscrutably. It was then up to the user to dig around in a manual, with no idea where to look.

Seasoned BASIC programmers will just chuckle and observe that his error was obvious. Sure, if you already know the language. But this was a *nontechnical* user, who only a day or so before took delivery on a long-awaited system in the hope that it would solve business problems. It will. But first he is going to have to painfully acquire enough "computer literacy" to make up for the machine's inadequacies.

For computers to become palatable to those who don't know or care about their hardware and software "innards," such system behavior must become a thing of the past. The makers of arcade games discovered this long ago: the machines that gobble the most quarters are the ones that can be learned well enough within one or two plays to provide a graceful evolution from naiveté to expertise, without requiring the user to consult a manual.

The only way all this can be translated into a specific recommendation is via the simple suggestion that you carefully observe the complexity of operator interaction required by whatever it is you are considering, and then match that to the patience, flexibility, available time, background, and intellectual resources of the people who will be using it.

7.3 FILE COMPATIBILITY

If you haven't already noticed by this time, the acquisition of a microsystem is subject to all sorts of little surprises. Some of them occur immediately; others lurk in the background for a year or two.

In the latter category, we have the small matter of file compatibility, not only with other systems, but with other programs running on your own. Some awareness of this can pay off well when, later, you want to transfer a text file to someone else's machine or expand your own operations.

Achieving file compatibility within your own system environment is not prohibitively difficult, as long as you keep that objective in mind when buying software. An oddball word processor, for example, might never be supported by such helpful tools as spelling checkers, indexing programs, footnote utilities, and information retrieval packages. WordStar, one of the preeminent standards at the moment, is supported by all four, and I can be reasonably certain that I am never to be stuck with a box of disks containing strange files that nothing else can read.

This issue takes on some interesting angles when we start thinking about more complex files such as those containing sales or accounting data. Are you committing thousands of hours of data-entry effort to a one-of-a-kind piece of bookkeeping software? What will happen when you finally get fed up with the lack of support and switch to a more standardized package?

Similar problems occur when you have occasion to transfer files from one machine to another, as I do when writing marketing literature for a client about 100 miles away. I just drop a disk containing WordStar text files in the mail, and he tinkers with the text as desired and then turns it into camera-ready copy.

But media-level compatibility isn't always possible. My last book, for example, made its way from these 8-inch floppies to whatever storage device was tied to the compositor's Digital Equipment Corporation VAX, via telephone. The VAX wouldn't have had the slightest idea what to do with a CP/M disk, so we skirted the issue and still managed to avoid manual reentry of the text by simply transmitting the whole manuscript over the Telenet communication network. Ain't technology wonderful?

7.4 MULTIUSER ENVIRONMENTS AND NETWORKING

Computers are *serial* devices, meaning that they can do only one thing at a time. This handicap is overcome somewhat with high speed, but it introduces some interesting problems when one attempts to use a single computer to perform simultaneous tasks.

It's quite possible, of course, as is evidenced by the preponderance of time-sharing systems out there that exist to do just that. But those, typically, offer more memory, more mass storage, and a lot of extra hardware to reduce the load on the CPU. To accomplish that sort of thing with a micro requires very careful design and some measure of care on the part of the user, even though the computer is probably spending well over 90% of its time sitting there waiting for someone to hit a key.

The problem arises when two users—such as one person printing payroll checks and another updating customer accounts—require system resources at the same time. Things get downright confusing if they are both trying to use the same *file*.

There are ways to handle the situation, all of which involve additional overhead. Some manufacturers just require a dedicated memory board for each user and deal with arbitration only when file accesses are performed. Others jump back and forth between tasks a few times each second whether they need to or not, and still others respond only to *interrupts* that indicate the need for attention to one of the tasks.

Whatever the approach, the problem is cumbersome in a typical microsystem, and this leads to a recommendation: if you need multiple users, provide multiple machines. This isn't quite as absurd as it sounds, for "local networking" techniques allow a number of systems to share infrequently needed (or particularly expensive) resources.

This rather neatly takes care of that overhead problem, for each user still has a dedicated system that won't "hang up" periodically to service another task. This is not always the case in traditional multiuser systems, which, if not properly designed, can become locked so thoroughly in the "deadly embrace" that they must be restarted from scratch.

The deadly embrace is a rather entertaining notion that lends some insight into the problems of designing a good multiuser system. In essence, it occurs when two users (or *tasks*)—say A and B—are running simultaneously and involved with closely related data. If two pieces of these data are called P and Q, the problem arises as follows: A has P and won't release it until it gets Q. B has Q and won't release it until it gets P. The tasks just sit there with their arms folded, glaring at each other.

Anyway, this sort of thing can be avoided through the use of multiple systems connected into a network. This permits all sorts of increases in efficiency, including "electronic mail" around the office, shared resources (such as expensive letter-quality printer), and simplified expansion down the road.

As shown in Figure 7-1, the local area network (in this case, the Corvus

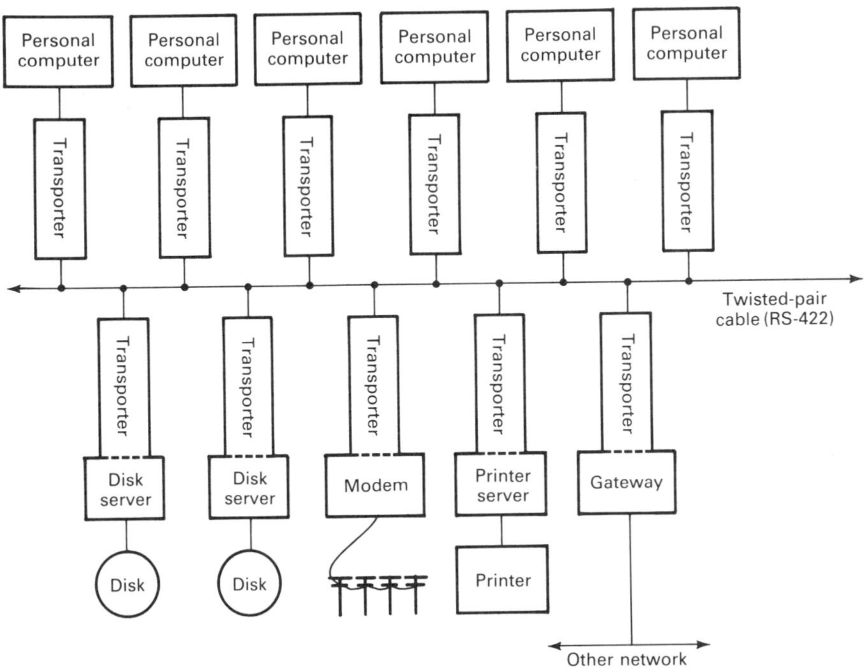

Figure 7-1 A local-area network permits a relatively unstructured relationship between numerous computers and support facilities. This is a much better way to ensure expandability than starting with a single big computer and adding more users. (Based on a drawing by Corvus Systems, Inc.)

Omninet) provides a means by which individual personal computers *(users)* can communicate with each other and with external computing resources *(servers)*. Data transfer takes place at the rate of 1 million bits per second, and the total length of the interconnecting line can be 4000 feet. In this case, the network consists of a simple twisted pair of wires, but other schemes may use more expensive (but faster) coaxial cable or optical fiber.

Each entity on the network, be it user or server, is interfaced via a simple piece of hardware known as a *transporter*. Whenever one unit wishes to send a message to another, its associated transporter waits for network availability, then transmits the message together with error-checking information, target address, special control codes, and other "communications overhead" items that are invisible to the user. If the message is not acknowledged by the recipient within a few microseconds, the sender waits a random amount of time and tries again. This continues, with the sender waiting a little longer each time, until the message has been satisfactorily transferred or until the system determines that the intended recipient is indeed dead.

Figure 7-2 The Corvus Omninet is often used to connect personal computers such as the IBM to mass storage units. (Courtesy of Corvus Systems, Inc.)

Other functions are performed by the transporters as well. They must be sensitive to *collisions*—cases when two units start talking simultaneously—as well as transmission errors. They must also accommodate equipment upgrades and later additions to the network.

Much of the beauty of networking lies in this flexibility. It is difficult to anticipate (or afford) all of your future system requirements when you are just getting started, and the use of a network (Figure 7-2) provides a cost-effective way to guarantee later flexibility. Most networking systems even permit interface to *other* networks, offering even more flexibility and letting you off the hook if the one you select turns out to be poorly supported a few years later.

7.5 PIRACY

The subject of microsystem management hardly seems to be an area in which a "cloak-and-dagger" issue such as piracy should surface, but surface it does. The problem is the unauthorized copying and distribution of software.

This phenomenon has become so widespread that software vendors have become seriously concerned about its effect on business and have, in fact, begun attempting to prosecute known offenders. But that's not particularly easy when it is necessary to invoke law enforcement agencies that are more concerned with violent crimes and those involving obvious sums of money. So what normally happens instead is an increase in the cost of software to cover a reduced market, encryption schemes, and stronger legal departments.

There's something very intangible about a program that makes it seem somehow okay to copy it. After all, you might reason, you certainly aren't *stealing* anything (the original still exists), and you probably aren't affecting the company's sales since you wouldn't have acquired the program in the first place if it had been necessary to pay the full price. So what's the harm in taking a copy of a friend's word-processing package home and using it for a little personal business (especially if you turned over a copy of your PL/I compiler in return)?

Well, the first sounds a lot like the old maternal "because I said so": it's illegal. Copyright laws unambiguously forbid reproduction of registered works, even if there is no intent to hustle them on the black market.

The second reason is moral: it really *is* stealing.

The third reason involves a sense of responsibility to the industry of which we are a part: even though prices seem unreasonably high, creation of a good software package can involve dozens of person-years. Someone has to pay for that, and if people won't, well, software quality won't be what it should be.

These things are pretty intangible when you're looking over your friend's shoulder at the neatest little spread-sheet package you've ever seen, especially when he says, "you want a copy of this?" Who could say "no"?

Of course, the odds of getting caught are small, but it is worth remembering that most robust software has a serial number built into it, often encrypted, that links it to the original purchaser. You can't file, peel, or grind it off. And this not only exposes you to charges of theft at any time in the future, but it also makes it damn hard to get any support from the vendor. If you are talking about a business application, you will be committing hundreds of thousands of hours to the system's integration with your work, making you somewhat vulnerable to a previously undetected bug.

The cost of legal purchase is thus often justified by support alone. Updates are issued to streamline operation or eliminate problems, a user's newsletter arrives periodically to pass along a few tricks and announce changes, and there's always the guy on the other end of the telephone line who can bail you out when you accidentally hit control-C in the middle of the year's most critical file update and desperately need to know how to recover. With pirated software, you orphan yourself, and that's a high price to pay even if the moral aspects *don't* bother you.

This whole issue has led to some entertaining battles between software vendors and pirates. For each progressively more esoteric encryption scheme, someone figures out a way to break it. Some are even marketed, such as the famous "Locksmith" program, which was itself pirated and sold at a reduced price by bootleggers . . . sort of a meta-piracy. By the time you read this, someone will probably be marketing a program that breaks the protection schemes employed by programs that break the protection schemes of still other programs that—well, you get the picture. It all becomes a game, you see.

One of the problems with this otherwise delightful intellectual exercise is that it becomes exceedingly difficult to make backup copies of your software for purely legitimate purposes. Earlier in the book and in the next chapter, we discuss the necessity of off-site backups, sacred masters, and so on, but they're making it hard to duplicate disks. An obvious solution is the purchase of backups, but that's expensive and basically absurd. There are too many levels of customization to be dealt with.

All this has led to customer complaints about the protection schemes, leading in turn to reversals of that policy and even recall of software packages that incorporate them. So we're back where we started.

The best recommendation is probably to just play it straight. You'll sleep better.

7.6 IN-HOUSE SOFTWARE DEVELOPMENT

Somewhere back in Chapter 1, during our discussion of vendor selection, we spoke of custom systems. That, obviously, can imply either hardware or software.

One thing we didn't talk about in that context is the development of custom software in your own business, either to address a particularly bizarre set of application requirements or to carve out a niche in the software market. After all, there *are* a lot of things that haven't been done yet, or are currently being done poorly.

Unfortunately, it's not a simple matter. In Section 6.2.2 we spoke of the distinction between "what" (this is, *what* I want the computer to do) and "how" (this is, exactly *how*). There is a temptation at the beginning of a software design project to put more emphasis on the first than the second. This is quite all right during the conceptualization phase, but it can lead to gross underestimations of the overall complexity of the task.

Software design is a complex mixture of art and engineering, with the insight and vision suggested by the former necessarily well supported by the structure and discipline of the latter. It looks easy. When a new user suddenly gets the hang of BASIC, he is often tempted to immediately get out of the lawn and garden business and hang out a shingle as a computer programmer. Actually, it *is* kind of easy, in a way, but a lot of work is required to produce a whole program that works reliably for all combinations of input data, recovers well from errors, protects itself against the abuses of the naive operator, is well documented, and offers the user enough flexibility to accommodate the inevitable oddball requirements.

If this isn't scary, and if you see in your own application a need that hasn't been adequately met by existing software packages, then go for it. But do so with a healthy respect for the myriad traps that lie in wait around the next bend.

8

Documentation and Organization

8.0 INTRODUCTION AND ALLEGRO

It is noble and necessary to address issues of human relationships, file security, user friendliness, and so on: these sorts of things comprise the cutting edge in the advancement of information technology. Great stuff. But somewhere in here we have to get down to the real nitty-gritty.

Below the aesthetic satisfaction of clever software design, the political intrigue of vendor relationships, and the interesting sociological questions of installing a computer in your business, there is a relentless, frustrating need for good organization. Not the kind of organization that inspires courses in MBA programs, but the kind that holds together hundreds of invisible disk files and pieces of obscure documentation, all of which change constantly.

This kind of organization doesn't really have any good parallels in the business world. Paper files (although certainly prone to clutter) aren't quite as subject to the whims of fate and magnetism as are their disk-resident counterparts. They are also less likely to disappear irrevocably upon issuance of a mistyped command, and even if all organization falls apart, they can at least be *read*.

But computers gain much of their charming mystery through the hosting of your critical information in a form that is in no way amenable to human senses. If the directory doesn't show your master customer list anymore, you just have to accept the fact that it's gone. You can't dig around in the disk to see if there's anything useful left (unless, of course, you like to get your hands dirty with maintenance utilities). No, you must accept the dictum of the machine.

In this kind of situation, you can't *afford* to be sloppy. Misplaced files, uncertain revision levels, documentation that doesn't match the current condition of the machine—all these can lead to more annoyance and confusion than all the other horrors in this book put together.

I would like to address some of these problems with a chapter full of recommendations. Together, they comprise a system that can accommodate a wide variety of application environments, and although it is inevitable that you will see deficiencies in the light of your own needs, they represent a useful starting point. This, indeed, is the Big Secret of system organization: start out with some kind of plan, lest things get out of hand before you even have a fighting chance.

8.1 PAPERWORK, MANUALS, AND FILING SYSTEMS

This sounds like pretty unglamorous stuff for a book on microsystem management, but even in the "paperless office' (if such a thing really exists), there is a need to keep track of system documentation, updates, revision levels, procedures, insurance information, listings of software, and so on. None of these things are particularly inspiring in the rosy flush of system acquisition, and as such, they usually constitute a pile on the corner of the desk.

But almost immediately, the pile starts to grow. Ads clipped from magazines mingle with computer store receipts and the thinner manuals. The stack is occasionally shuffled as items are sought, but it generally takes on a last-in, first-out form as the stuff at the bottom gradually becomes inapplicable to present reality.

Eventually, the pile is caught up in a whirlwind cleanup campaign in anticipation of some auspicious visit, and the chaos is in full swing. Now, finding a necessary piece of information involves not only a riffle through the *new* stack already growing on the desk, but also a trip around the room to visit the others that have propagated as if by magic.

There must be a better way.

8.1.1 The Computer Room File Cabinet

Such piles of paper are such a pain to work around that some attention up front—even before system installation—should be given over to the creation of a special filing system for the computer room. In most microsystem installations, a single drawer is quite sufficient, incorporating all but the business files (financial reports, manuscripts, mailing lists, or whatever) generated by the system. The idea here is the establishment of an organizational scheme by which you can keep track of the system itself.

One good way to approach this problem (which is larger than it looks—if you don't believe it, just let the piles form and *then* try to get organized) is to partition the file drawer into four distinct sections. These, in turn, are made up of as many individual files as are necessary to keep everything straight (Figure 8-1). Let's look at these four sections and their probable contents:

- **HARDWARE DOCUMENTATION.** Much of this is automatically taken care of by the manuals that were presumably provided with the system. But there are a few other things that need to be kept available for future reference. Purchase records, for example, could come in handy in the event of equipment loss or failure. The first file should contain copies of your receipts, warranty information with the registration dates noted, and a list of all equipment serial numbers. Since this is the sort of thing that would come in handy in the event of fire, photocopies of these things should also be in your safe deposit box.

  This *Purchase Records* file is also a good place for quotes from vendors on anticipated purchases, tax information, depreciation schedules, and all that.

  A second hardware file is *Support,* which should contain a list of the names and phone numbers of knowledgeable people at the various manufacturers represented by the system. (This being a topsy-turvy business, it's good to update the list frequently.) This file might also contain merchandise return forms, together with the names of a few local experts and some nearby users of the same equipment. These are the things that can spell the difference between sanity and madness when your machine inexplicably goes belly-up in the middle of a critical operation.

  Third, a file called *Modifications* can be invaluable. As you accrue more and more experience with the system, you may find yourself installing all sorts of little patches and changes that in one way or another enhance its operation. Some are strictly for convenience, like a remote reset switch for those systems that only offer one on the back panel; others are recommended by the manufacturer in order to correct a design problem. In all cases, even the simple ones, a notation should

THE COMPUTER ROOM FILE CABINET

HARDWARE DOCUMENTATION

Purchase Records	Support
Modifications	Things to Do
Configuration	--------
--------	--------
--------	--------
--------	--------
(specific hardware files)	--------
--------	--------

MAINTENANCE

Maintenance Log	Preventive Maintenance
Media Life Records	Questions & Problems

SOFTWARE DOCUMENTATION

I/O Drivers	Revision Log
Memory Map	Questions & Problems
Backup Log	Master File Directory
Procedures	--------
--------	--------
--------	--------
--------	--------
(specific software files)	--------
--------	--------

LIBRARY

Magazine Indices	Database Info
--------	--------
--------	--------
--------	--------
(specific articles)	--------
--------	--------

Figure 8-1 A good organizational start in planning a computer room is the creation of a filing system that can accommodate the growth, changes, and problems of the machine.

be made and deposited in the modifications file. Somebody—probably you—will appreciate it later.

The fourth file in the hardware section might be called *Things to Do*. This should never get very full, for it is just a temporary repository of patches and changes that need to be made next time the system is shut down and somebody is feeling ambitious. As I write, my system is awaiting a replacement fan filter, the installation of a "Glitch-Guard" for power-glitch protection, a "paper-out override" switch for the printer, and a modification to the CRT that will allow easier conversion from word processing to on-line terminal operation. These all take the form of random notes in the fourth hardware file.

Fifth, there should be a file that accurately documents the present system *Configuration*. What boards are installed? What are the I/O port assignments? How many spare edge connectors are there on the bus? How is the whole mess cabled, and what are the settings of all those "dipswitches" that tell the computer, the terminal, and the printer what baud rates and communications options to use? If the system goes out for service, or if you move it to another location, an unambiguous sketch of all this can prevent considerable frustration.

After these five files, the rest is a function of the specific installation. There can be any number of files detailing the various elements of the system: kit plans, schematics, manufacturer correspondence, skinny manuals on various peripherals, disk drive documentation, and so on. (I mention *skinny* manuals because the fat ones are probably on a shelf somewhere. The others tend to get lost)

Together, this collection of hardware files represents an up-to-date image of your machine. When you have problems, try to sell it, or wish to add to it, this information can be of tremendous assistance. But there's more.

- **MAINTENANCE.** Immediately following the hardware section in the file cabinet, there should be four maintenance files.

First, and most important, is the *Maintenance Log*. We discussed this briefly back in Section 3.2.1: by providing an organized collection of comments about system problems and fixes, the maintenance log allows future problem diagnosis to become progressively easier. After a while, patterns tend to develop, and the solution that once required three hours of expensive deliberation might only take ten minutes the second time—*if* somebody thought to make a record of it. This can be more than a time- and money-saver: it can help create a convincing case against a vendor of flaky hardware. Few people feel confident arguing against solid documentation.

The second file in this section should be called *Preventive Main-*

tenance (PM). This one is a must: printers need to be lubricated, filters and heads need to be cleaned, disk drives need to be aligned, and some systems have components that require periodic calibration (analog I/O and the like). In the complacency of trouble-free use, it is easy to forget all this tedious stuff until three years have passed without a drop of oil in the printer and the bearings suddenly need replacement. If you take the time during system installation to collect all the various manufacturers' recommendations concerning preventive maintenance and make appropriate notations on a calendar, the work is more likely to get done.

Third, this section needs some scheme for keeping track of *media life*. Diskettes fail. Although a detailed record of media acquisition dates is not, by itself, of much use, it is a good starting point for some rough records that can suggest amid the complacency of trouble-free operation that a disk needs to be retired. In a typical situation, one piece of media called "the system disk" is inserted in Drive A, where it stays until, many months later, it suddenly and tragically goes over the hill with a nonrecoverable error. This sort of thing can be prevented by copying the heavily used disks every three to six months and sending them to a retirement home on the back of your media shelf. Don't pitch them—an unforeseen crash may render them suddenly critical.

Anyway, file 3 in the maintenance section should provide a means of keeping records about all this, perhaps in the form of a simple list of diskette numbers with space for notes.

The last file in this section is *Questions and Problems*. Periodic conversations with the manufacturer are much more productive if you have a list of questions in front of you while you talk. It seems trivial, but you will inevitably notice irregularities that should be brought to someone's attention but don't justify an immediate call: these are things that can easily be forgotten without being noted somewhere.

- **SOFTWARE.** The point of the whole system, of course, is the execution of programs that in one fashion or another enhance the activity of your business. As such, any documentation scheme applied to your installation should include a well-thought-out scheme for keeping track of software manuals, updates, revisions, procedures, implementation notes, glitches, flaws, patches, correspondence, reviews, advertisements, and registration materials.

  This can be quite a headache, especially in a dynamic installation where things change constantly. In such situations, it becomes doubly important to document a system configuration that works so that you can readily recover from changes that don't.

  A good start is a file called *I/O Drivers*. It is not at all uncommon for an unusual printer (or an oddball pair of disk drives like mine) to require a somewhat different I/O scheme than that which was shipped with your operating system. There's nothing dismaying about this, of course, until you upgrade to a new version of the system and find yourself wondering how to make it work. The solution is to keep extensive notes about the I/O driver patches in this file, enabling, at the very least, someone to figure out a new approach based on the one that worked originally. As a general rule, every change to standard software puts you totally on your own, far from the assistance or even sympathy of the original vendor.

It's quite okay for vendors to make all the changes they want, of course; those are called *revisions*. They appear on your doorstep at odd intervals, bearing new features, fixes of old problems, and strange new numbers that flash on the screen at sign-on time. This is all very exciting, but before performing a wholesale replacement of the corresponding files on all your disks, it is a good idea to write-protect a couple of the older versions and store them, then make a list of the disks to be upgraded for the *Revision Log* file. This same file should have a record, in some convenient form, of the revision numbers of all pieces of software present in your installation. This apparent bit of trivia can become critically important when you need help from the vendor or when you start noticing that files created under one revision of a particular program can't be read under another.

The third file in the software section should be a *Memory Map*. This is a rough drawing of the system's "address space," showing the regions occupied by the operating system, the I/O drivers, a running job, text, the stack, ROM area, memory-mapped I/O devices, and so on. When you are adding a patch and looking for a safe area for a storage buffer, this will help. You can get away without this if you plan to avoid tinkering, but it's not a bad idea to have an image of memory use in your head anyway.

Like the maintenance section, the software section needs a file called *Questions and Problems*. The rationale is the same: during normal operation, you are bound to notice strange things that may or may not be problems. If you jot a quick note and throw it in this file, you can establish a pattern, clear up the problem entirely, or collect enough questions to justify a call to your friendly software vendor.

The fifth one is very important, and grows more so with every day that you use your system. It is the *Backup Log*. In Section 8.2 we'll have more to say about this, but in essence, its purpose is the establishment of a record that lets you find copies of files that have abruptly given in to the various horrors we have discussed throughout this book. Does your customer master file yield only a "BDOS ERR ON B: BAD SECTOR" or similarly chilling message whenever you try to read it? Don't despair; just grab the backup copy. This wouldn't require a special file folder, but for the fact that you will probably end up with quite a few backups and they can get just as lost as anything else.

The backup log is closely allied with the *Master File Directory,* one of the most useful printed listings you are likely to find in a computer room. It is nothing more than an occasional printout of the directories of *all* of your disks (by number or other code), enabling you to find—although perhaps inefficiently—any file you own. I say "inefficiently" because an unsorted listing of thousands of files is nothing short of a nuisance, but there will inevitably be some ancient and obsolete relics stashed in the back of the diskette box that you suddenly need, and there might as well be a less painful way to find them than manually doing a directory of each disk. There is some software on the market that does all this for you, and if you spend a lot of time looking for old files, it might be worth investigating. (The best approach is to dispense with floppies entirely and use a large enough hard disk system to host everything—backed up, of course.)

The next file in this section is simply *Procedures,* and contains nothing more than the written sequences of steps for some of those infrequently needed but critical operations (such as formatting disks, installing a new revision of the operating system, and so on). These things are usually described in a manual somewhere, but it is convenient to have notes describing procedures that not only actually work, but also take your own system's pecularities into account.

The rest of the software section is made up of as many files as are necessary to describe all the programs available to your system. As noted earlier, most applicable information in this category takes the form of manuals and binders, but there are usually a few other things—spare reference cards, revision notes, published reviews, and so on—that are of interest. Whenever adding a new software package to your installation, just create a corresponding file folder. Something will land in it sooner or later. One file can even be a catchall for random routines that look like they might be interesting someday.

- **THE COMPUTER ROOM LIBRARY.** No computer room is complete without a few shelves overflowing with magazines, binders, and books about everything from programming in a baroque style to microsystem management. It's the magazines that cause trouble.

In one year, eight subscriptions to monthlies, two to biweeklies, one to a weekly, and a few random newsstand purchases total over 200 copies of potentially useful publications. Which issue offered that neat little trick for increasing the speed of batch file execution under CP/M?

It is not enough to simply order them all by date and keep them in neat stacks, although that certainly improves their appearance. And you certainly can't throw them away . . .

What's needed, ideally, is a massive data base of their contents that you can search on the basis of keywords in order to produce a bibliographic reference. As it turns out, this is quite possible with available techniques (as long as you don't mind either on-line connect charges of about $1 per minute or the amount of human time necessary to build and maintain a local data base instead).

The cheap alternative, crude though it may be, is the creation of some file folders called *Magazine Indices* (by year or by magazine, depending on your inclination). Within them, paper-clipped into convenient groups, are photocopies of the index pages of all your magazines and/or the annual indices that some publications provide. These can be annotated as necessary to flag items of potential interest, yielding a crude but effective cross-reference to all that tonnage on the shelves. Allied with this can be as many clippings files as you like, implying either exuberant use of the copier or the decimation of your magazine collection.

Trying to keep all this up to date is certainly a nuisance, but it's worth at least a token effort. It pays for itself the first time a hastily retrieved article solves a problem that might have otherwise called for a consultant.

8.2 SYSTEM FILES

Enough paperwork. The whole business of computing involves the manipulation of data, and at least for the present, that is dependent on files. We have already spoken somewhat about the nature of files—how they are created and destroyed, how they are found via a directory, and how they are made to optimally occupy the scattered space available on a disk. Fortunately, we have computers to keep track of all that.

It is a little trickier, however, to get the computer to *organize* the files that seem to proliferate madly whenever someone so much as looks at the terminal. For example, suppose that there was a nice little autobiographical sketch in a letter you wrote last year with the word processor, and you want it now for a proposal. Where is it? In which of those 114 floppies on the shelf might you find that file, the name of which you can't quite recall? What do you do, print 114 directories and then look at all the plausible-sounding text? It might be easier to just start over.

This sort of thing is obviously maddening, and it can be expensive in terms of more than human time. Lost software, accidentally erased backups of financial data, expensive boilerplate that must be recreated by your attorney; none of these are uncommon in the microsystem world. You come to hate floppy disks after a while, even if you are lucky enough to remain free of media failures.

"Easy," you might say. "Just get a hard disk and be done with all the confusion." Sorry. Even a hard disk of infinite size, while certainly eliminating the nuisance of floppies, leaves unaffected the problem of files that proliferate with every system activity. In fact, the seductive freedom of all that space tempts some users to save everything, yielding in short order a confusing jumble of files that lack even the artificial boundaries of diskette jackets to impose some sort of order. You can at least label a floppy with something like

```
THE COMPLETE GUIDE TO MICROSYSTEM MANAGEMENT (MS71)
                    Disk 2 of 4
```

and stash it safely away from everything else.

It is clear that any kind of dynamic installation (that's anyplace that has a computer, ac power, and at least one human being) can profit immeasurably from some kind of organizational scheme designed to keep track of disk files. This can range from the simple "master directory listing" extracted once every month or so to a sophisticated software package that allows files to be automatically located via logical relationships between keywords. The complexity of the application and the amount of data left in its wake determine the amount of effort that somebody, or something, needs to expend on an ongoing basis to keep it all straight. Let's have a look at some techniques that can be applied to assist with this.

8.2.1 Filenaming Conventions

The first step is to decide up front how you are going to name your files. This sounds rather trivial, but it is the heart of many an organizational scheme (and even if you have no scheme at all, this can establish the "bottom line" of file-hunting difficulty).

Systems of various styles differ widely in the methods by which file names can be established. Some, like the hardy perennial called CP/M and its various hybrid offspring, allow filenames of up to eight characters, followed by an optional one- to three-character extension separated from the rest by a period. Others eschew the extension and depend instead on a numeric "file type" designator. Operating systems of the UNIX class, in a significant departure from this traditional philosophy, permit a "tree" structure in which each complete filename includes not only the file label itself, but also a sequence of names that describe a succession of branches leading all the way back through the system to what is, naturally, called the root. Even without exploring the sublime organizational pleasures to be had in such an environment, it is clear that there's a substantial difference. More deliciously different still are "object-oriented" computing environments based on new languages such as Smalltalk. But whatever the operating system structure, it is still up to the user to impart some kind of intellectual order to the megabytes of data that accumulate.

Perhaps the easiest way to approach this, especially in those systems that permit the use of extensions, is simply to adopt a protocol that governs the assignment of filenames. This may be handled more or less automatically in a turnkey software package such as an integrated accounting system, but if you are working in any environment that allows you to choose names for your files, a simple protocol can go a long way toward keeping things straight.

The first step is to create a list of three-character extensions, together with their meanings. In my system, for example, I use the following standards:

ADV Advertising copy
ASM Assembler source file
BAK WordStar or line-editor backup file
BAS BASIC source file
BZO BASIC/Z object file
BZS BASIC/Z source file
CMD Command (batch) file
COM Executable command file
FOR FORTRAN source file
FRM Business form
HEX Intel HEX format object file
INV Invoice
LBL Text for printed labels

LIB Library file

LSP LISP source file

LTR Letter

MST Format specification master file

nnn Manuscript number ‘nn’ or disk number ‘nnn’ if the label is @@@ (see the text)

OLD Text file copied from previous system, still in old format

OUT Outline

OVL (or OVR) Program overlay file

PRN Printer or listing file

QRY Query letter

REL Relocatable object file

SYM Symbol table from the assembler

TXT Random text

Z80 Z-80 assembler source file

and so on. This provides an unambiguous set of specific categories into which all disk files must fall (some of them, in fact, are required or created by system programs).

In some cases, this isn't quite convenient, however, such as a book manuscript that consists of a number of chapters. No problem—I just use the extension to keep track of the revision number. This file, for example, is called CGM8.5, for *The Complete Guide to Microsystem Management*, Chapter 8, version five. This highlights one invariant feature of any kind of adopted convention: it is not invariant.

That takes care of the filename's extension, but what about the rest of it? In most systems, you have an average of eight characters to play with (although Apples, for example, offer a 20-character field in which extensions are optional), and it is a good idea to take full advantage of this. Instead of such ambiguous filenames as NOTES.TXT or ARTICLE.138, try using words that will suggest the content of the file when you see them in the directory a year later, such as AI-CONF.TXT, MEDLINE.138, or CUST-LIST.DAT.

So far this is all pretty obvious, and quite comparable to the commonsense approach to choosing names for the labels on manila file folders. But this is only the beginning. The next step is the establishment of some kind of system that integrates your named files into a cohesive order. The nature of this system is entirely dependent on your operation: in my case, for example, it makes sense to let each disk carry files generated over a specific period of time, as opposed to a scheme that would require a disk swap for every kind of task (articles, letters, invoices, etc). But many people find it much more efficient to draw fixed boundaries between disks and keep different classes of files forever separate.

No matter which method proves to be best, it will quickly spawn a number of disks bearing files of current interest. This is a classic nuisance, and demands the establishment of a system to keep them all straight. There are two basic ways to do this. The disks can be serial-numbered, then cross-referenced as necessary. This tends to work well with my approach, where a given disk is likely to remain relatively undisturbed in a drive for a month or more. The other method takes good advantage of those little colored labels that always come with a box of floppies: create a few categories and then stick with them as much as possible. General business applications that involve numerous data disks for payroll, general ledger, inventory, word processing, and so on, seem to justify this approach far more than does my rather sharply focused use.

In either case, the disks should be unambiguously identified, both by the gummed label on the outside and by a machine-readable file inside. I have found one technique to be of particular value: Each disk has a serial number, which becomes part of the filename for a "disk ID" file. A typical filename (this disk, for example) is "@@@ .29". The disk number is 29, and the "@@@" assures that this label will always be the first one in an alphabetized file directory.

The content of the file is updated whenever I feel inspired to do a little maintenance. At the moment, it reads:

```
DISK # 29
Mfr: Dysan 3740/2D
Vendor: Royal Data–1/5/82
CP/M version: SR/D
Formatted: 7/22/82
BADLIM last run: 8/10/82–OK
Burps: none yet

CONTENTS:  Miscellaneous Text Files (WS) MS71 (7 and 8)
```

Over time, this little file will accumulate comments about problems, heaviness of use, date of retirement from active service, and generalities about the disk's file content. This will be useful in determining just how long I can press my luck with it in full-time use and in helping me select future media vendors (if Brand X seems to last half as long as Brand Z, and Brand Z costs only 25% more than Brand X, you know which one I'll buy).

The disk ID file also appears on the master directory list, an eminently useful adjunct to any other file management scheme. (This is the printout, produced at regular intervals, of the file directories of all disks in the computer room.)

The value of this is considerable. Even in relatively static system environments, things are changing constantly. There is a frequent need to locate a file that is not in current use—for any of a number of reasons—and one simple way to accomplish this without the overhead of fancy systems is a simple hard copy of all your directories. No, they're not cross-reference, but at least they're there. Much can be said for that. The more complex the organizational scheme, the more work it takes to keep it current (an exception, perhaps, is an automatically maintained system supported by the computer).

Creating the master directory list is a tedious but simple task: just insert all your disks, one by one, into a drive. For each one, print the disk ID file and a directory, then move on to the next. Then date it, drop it into the *Master File Directory* folder described in the software part of Section 8.1, and you're done. It'll pay off.

The key to all these nuisance tasks involving files is simply the creation and maintenance of some kind of system that is well suited to your application. Like manual small-business accounting schemes, which range from a couple of three-ring notebook pages to a double-entry general ledger in fancy post binders, file management techniques can be as simple or complex as you like. It is best to avoid the exceedingly complex unless it is justified, and/or you can afford the clerical help to maintain it.

8.2.2 Backups and Revisions

This is one of those areas where a little bit of negligence can go a long way. Unlike organizational schemes where the cost of sloppiness is mere inefficiency, the management of file backups is critical to the survival of your data.

If you recall our horror stories of Chapter 2, you will have a sobering image of disks as capricious temporary repositories for data, subject like nothing else in the world to the whims of heat, magnetism, dust, finger oils, wear, smoke, cat hair, manufacturing defects, abusive disk drives, and pure chance. That's a reasonable view. And although disks routinely survive years of intermittent use, it becomes progressively harder to depend on them as time passes. Some people do, and manage to get away with it.

Adding to all this is the ongoing frantic development pace of an industry that seems hell-bent on tracking the exponential development curve of storage density no matter what, while in many cases, the "what" is a propensity for low reliability. I have recently engaged in protracted battle with a major West Coast drive manufacturer, one of the first to offer "half-height" 8-inch floppy disk drives. The issue centered on poor performance, accelerated media wear, and thermal sensitivity in what is otherwise a very exciting product for this particular point in the industry's growth. Had I remained content with the boring old single-sided, single-density, slow, power-gulping clunkers, I would be blissfully unaware of media problems. But like everyone else, I found the established standards to be painfully restrictive once I got wind of the new models.

We can do more about this than complain and publish negative product reviews. A well-maintained, deliberate backup system should render the occasional disk error little more than a nuisance. Establishing this is a matter of some planning and management, but it is well within practical reach of most small system users. Let's consider it on two levels.

First, and simplest, is what we may call the *casual file backup* technique. If your application is, say, general-purpose word processing, you probably generate a lot of files that are not particularly important once they have been printed. Nestled in there are doubtless a few that are very important, however, and you need a way to protect yourself against their loss without troubling yourself with all the letters and memos that are overdue for deletion anyway.

The trick is simply producing copies of whatever important files you possess, making sure that they are on another disk stored safely away from the others. This is deceptively trivial.

Actually, it *is* trivial for those files that never, or rarely, change. In this category are the various system utility programs, boilerplate text, standard forms, and so on. But what about, say, a book, manual, or program that is under continuous development? How about a customer mailing list, a data base of subcontractors, or a slowly growing spelling dictionary? (I'm leaving inventory and accounting out of this for reasons that will become clear shortly.)

These files need to be backed up too, but keeping track of which version the backup represents may prove difficult. One thing must therefore be done: associate a revision code or date with the file, and make sure it also appears in the backup, preferably in the filename. You may have noticed in the preceding section, for example, that the file for this chapter was called CGM8.5 (Chapter 8, version 5). Actually, it is now CGM8.6, and on another disk across the room may be found a file called BCGM8.5. This is distinguished from the ".BAK" files generated by the word processor, which are simply the *previous* versions with their filename extensions changed. Hardly sufficient, after a few hours' writing.

Another file around here that is updated two or three times a month is the one containing a summary of my portfolio—a useful marketing tool. The present version is called CREDITS.O6B, being the second version in the sixth month. There's little need for historical tracking of these, so I simply make sure after each edit that the file is copied to another disk, again safely away from the computer area (not that I'm paranoid, you understand, but anything is possible).

Clearly, doing things this way is a bit haphazard, and depends for its success on the user's initiative in maintaining the backup files. It is rather a pain, and often doesn't get done. But the overhead is low, and with the aid of some "archiving" system utilities, it becomes almost easy.

The second major technique for assuring yourself of file security, however, takes on a life of its own. Generally considered more appropriate for accounting, inventory, payroll, mailing list, and software development systems, this method involves the backup of *entire disks* at fixed intervals. No longer is the first comment on file loss: "Oh no, I hope I backed that up somewhere!" With this method, you can be assured that all data up to last Friday (or last night, or last whatever) is safely tucked away on one of a rotating series of three sets of backup disks.

It works like this: at fixed intervals (let's assume weekly), a backup procedure is undertaken as suggested by Figure 8-2. As shown, there are three disks (or groups of disks) that take turns being the working version, the primary backup, and the secondary backup. At the end of the week, the data from A is copied onto C, which was the backup from two weeks before. A then becomes the primary backup, and C becomes the working version. Meanwhile, B moves into position as the secondary backup, ready to become the working version on the following week.

It may appear confusing at first glance, but it is really quite elegant. The disks all take turns on center stage, a feature that is more than just fair play. They all receive equal wear, and the process of copying (if done on a file-by-file rather than a disk-image basis) efficiently "packs" the data, which may be spread all over the disk. Also, you are not out on a limb if something tragic happens in the process of making the copy, since you can always go back two weeks instead of one and reconstruct.

It is wise to plan for this reconstruction. In a safe somewhere, on paper, there should be an audit trail of raw transactions (whatever they are). This will allow complete restoration of the present status should one of your disks fail.

Note, by the way, what would happen if only two disks were involved in the backup procedure, instead of three. If there were just A and B, and they took turns every week, imagine your dismay if some critical file developed a problem about which you were unaware. At backup time, that

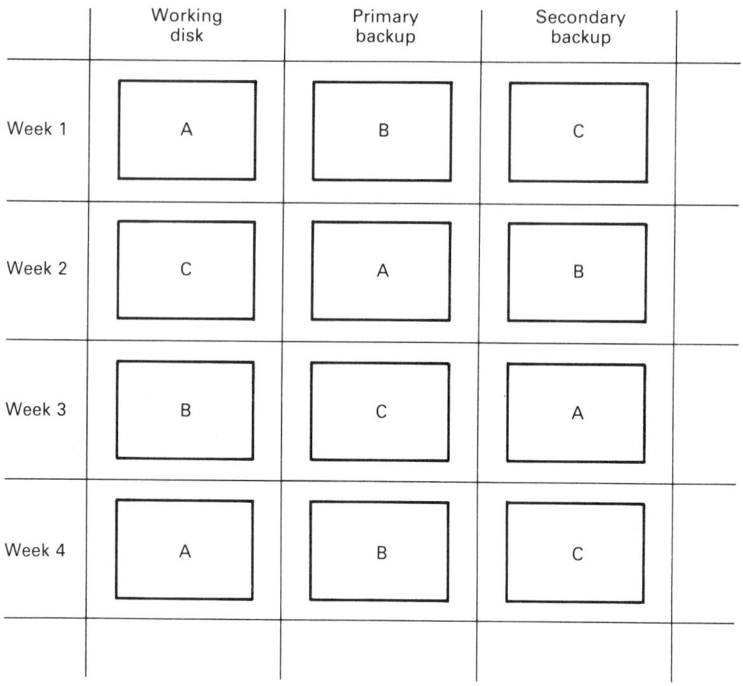

Figure 8-2 The "grandfather" backup scheme involves rotation of disks to ensure even wear and easy availability to the previous two weeks' data if the current disk fails.

bad file would be copied over your only good file, and any chance of reconstruction would be lost. There should *always* be three disks, or sets of disks, involved in a backup scheme. This is often called the "grandfather" method.

The purpose of the backups, of course, is to provide insurance in the event of a work disk failing in service. But before rushing to the safe, grabbing the primary backup, and shoving it into the drive so you can get back to work, *make a copy!* There is a possibility that the problem is in your disk drive, and it wouldn't do to destroy your insurance. Always try to keep in mind the number of hours that would be required to reconstruct everything by hand, and protect yourself.

There's another class of backups that needs to be considered somewhere in here. Your original-issue software, representing an investment of perhaps thousands of dollars, is one of those things that should be insured as well. But there's little point in making weekly copies; that just ties up disk space with something that doesn't change.

The basic idea is to simply copy the disk when it arrives, then store it safely away from everything else and work with the copy. But there's a potential problem with this that I mentioned back in Chapter 3: disk drives can gradually drift out of alignment, rendering the original-issue software quite unreadable a year or two after installation. This is especially insidious if you have been following the grandfather backup method, for you will remain blissfully unaware of any problem until you need to dip into the "sacred master" box for some reason and find that read errors proliferate. The solution to this is to make two copies of original issue software instead of one.

The original still gets stashed away, untouched. But the copies are rotated every six months, including a reformatting operation. This takes care of gradual alignment drift and assures you of a reasonably good match between the working disk and the drive.

It follows from this that similar concerns arise with the rotating group of three backups that house your data. Indeed. They should be retired every six months or so, and kept in a separate box as scratch disks or low-priority backups.

It is obvious from all this that the term "management" in this context is not misplaced. One of the first things that needs to be done when a new system is brought on-line is the creation of a schedule for backup management, and the assignment of a person to the task. This person should be required to sign a checklist for each week's procedure, helping to assure that this "weekly hassle" gets done without fail. Good records might even induce an understanding insurance underwriter to give you a break on your rates.

Before leaving this subject, we need to explore one more backup-related item: off-site storage. This can take two forms. First, and simplest, is the acquisition of a safe-deposit box wherein copies of your sacred masters and weekly backups are kept. The advisability of this is entirely a function of your operation, but even in a fairly casual environment, a trip to the lockbox every month or so is not a bad idea. Fire, you know.

The second type of off-site backup involves the use of another computer, with an occasional file transmission over the telephone. I have frequently done this with book files, after the sheer mass of text begins to frighten me with its essential volatility. Ideally, you can find a friend with some free disk space to trade, but failing that, commercial services such as the Source or CompuServe will happily rent you file space for a nominal monthly charge. This can give you a very secure feeling: not only are your data stored off-site, but they're even in a different city!

This section is entitled "Backups and Revisions," and so far we have only talked about the former. We can take *revisions* to mean changes in software files, either generated in a development environment or provided by the software vendor. In a strict sense, every change in an active data file is a revision, but that's a rather different matter.

The reason that revisions are something of an issue is that they generally represent updates or "fixes" of problems, and thus should be implemented throughout your system as they become available. There can be problems, however: sometimes there can be compatibility problems from one revision to the next, or more commonly, the other way around. A new version of your accounting system should therefore be tried with some caution, and the old sacred master should be left alone just in case.

Hopefully, this sort of thing won't create difficulty, and there will be nothing to worry about but the matter of smoothly implementing the revision. This basically involves little more than a few file transfer operations, but many future headaches will be prevented if you make certain that the revision number appears in the filename. Strange old files sometimes surface during the excitement of intense computer use, and if there *are* "downward-compatibility" problems, somebody's going to be mighty confused if there is no obvious indication that PAYROLL.COM is not the same as PAYROLL.COM. System disks should be labeled on the outside with the revision number of all software contained within them, together with the date and other pertinent information.

With that, we arrive at one last category of file-organizing tools.

8.2.3 Automatic File-Management Systems

One of the holy grails of the microcomputer software business throughout its adolescence was the successful development of a system that would enable a user to locate files anywhere in his disk library without having to riffle through them or read a master directory listing. This turned out to be more complex than it sounded (to do it well, anyway), and the few schemes that appeared on the market were little more than rudimentary data base packages that helped cross-reference file names and disk numbers. They were potentially useful, but imposed quite a bit more practical overhead than doing it the old-fashioned way.

The limiting factor was not human cleverness; it was storage capacity. For such an idea to become practical, it must always be resident in the system, must be automatically updated by all activity, and must allow the user to find files not just by name, but by content. "Where's that letter I wrote to the folks in London about reimbursement for conference expenses?" If this kind of system can be created, microcomputers can take another microstep out of the dark ages.

It's happening. Systems such as the Swedish "SAF" and others of their ilk allow the use of free-text filenames and maintain a built-in data base of *all words* in all files. With the exception of a list of declared "nonwords," all the words in each new file are alphabetized and merged into a master file, where they point to whatever text files in the system (on any disk) they came from. In the example above, I might enter "London" and be advised by the system that 18 files have contained that word. Refining it, I type "and conference" and find that three files contain both. Finally, "and reimburs?" pins it down to one, on disk 44 (the question mark takes care of uncertainty about the final letters of the word; did I say "please reimburse me" or "I request reimbursement"?).

This sort of thing is still a pain with floppies, primarily because they are intrinsically slow. But a decent hard disk, now commonplace, can host a healthy data base like this without bogging down or hogging all your space. It's worth considering.

A moment's rhapsody: as this technology grows further and further away from its tortured infancy (in which people actually maintained customer data bases on *cassette tape*!), it is becoming more and more possible to actually use computers as tools outside the specific applications areas for which widely marketed programs exist. We have always had to pay the price of high overhead to take advantage of sophisticated features (someday we'll read history books and marvel at the dedication of people who actually accepted the need to handle magnetic media just so they could use those primitive machines). But mass memory is getting cheaper and denser, making *huge* programs reasonable, and we're already seeing videodiscs in archival storage applications (108,000 video frames on a single platter).

I mention all this as something of a philosophical disclaimer. We're not going to be saddled with current technology forever, and some of the tedium of system management gives way with every significant advance. Robust minicomputers such as DEC's VAX, for example, routinely handle revision management and automatic journaling without requiring the attention of the user; it is obvious that such features will continue to be encompassed by micros as they deliver, each year, more bang for the proverbial buck.

9

Supplies, Accessories, and Gadgets

9.0 INTRODUCTION

Like cameras, sailboats, and bicycles, computers tend to become considerably more expensive over time than their sticker prices would seem to suggest. This is attributable to the need for supplies and accessories, ranging from obvious consumable items such as paper, ribbon, and diskettes to power-line monitors, printer stands, decollators, paper shredders, printwheel cleaning kits, electronic copyholders, and all those add-on pieces of hardware and software advertised almost everywhere you look. You can spend as much as you want.

Not all accessories are as universally necessary as the ads suggest, however, and it is the purpose of this chapter to bring some order to the microsystem "aftermarket" by categorizing and discussing some of the myriad items available.

I might note, first, that the industry has spawned a number of preeminent companies whose primary business is selling items of this sort. It is definitely worthwhile to get yourself on some of the mailing lists (the addresses are given in Appendix A).

Now, let's take a look at the wealth of goods available to spruce up your computer room. To impart some order to a rather large subject, I have created four categories: media and accessories, printer supplies and accessories, furniture and computer room items, and miscellaneous accessories and gadgets.

9.1 MEDIA AND ACCESSORIES

Throughout this book, we have given much space to the various problems associated with magnetic storage media, expounding at length on matters ranging from their organization to their protection. Now we can consider the media market a bit, as well as a number of products that have evolved to make the foregoing matters somewhat easier to deal with.

You can find floppy disks anywhere within a roughly 3 : 1 price range, with the difference being a function of manufacturing quality, marketing, sleeve design, sectoring, and suitability for extended-range operation (double-sided, double-density, double-tracking, and so on). Some mighty tantalizing ads appear regularly in the computer magazines, but whenever you are tempted by an unbelievable bargain, just remember the *real* cost of a disk if it fails prematurely in service.

Sad but true, it is possible to buy a box of ten disks, take it home, and discover that only six or seven of them can be formatted without error. Even if they were so cheap that you still win on a price-per-disk basis, this hardly inspires confidence. I can personally attest to the fact that creative effort is inhibited if you distrust the system. The cheapest disks you can own are the ones that always work.

The major mail-order computer supply firms, such as Inmac and Uarco, include in their catalogs a disk-selection guide to help you pick the medium that's right for your system. Computer stores, of course, also carry disks to fit the machines they sell, and they are even showing up in book, hobby, and department stores. By the time you read this, there will probably be displays of floppy disks to tempt impulse buyers at grocery store checkout counters.

Disk cartridges and packs for removable-media hard disk systems are another matter. These are seldom discounted deeply, and I have yet to see any truly tacky off-brand units. Part of the reason for this is the fact that manufacturing tolerances on hard disk media are so tight that not just anyone can bang them together. The prices reflect this, ranging (depending on the model) from about $50 to over $1500.

Similar comments can be made about magnetic tape (the kind on reels, not cassettes), but we would rapidly move away from the microsystem world with talk about *that*.

9.1.1 Diskette Storage and Filing Systems

One of the more necessary accessories in the computer room is some method of storing your disks or other media. For a while, you can get away with the little cardboard boxes that they come in, but it doesn't take long for that to become annoying. No problem: if there's anything that all the computer supply depots have in common by now, it's a stock of floppy storage accessories.

But there's tremendous diversity (Figure 9-1). Let's consider the options. Simplest, perhaps, are the plastic floppy storage boxes that are just

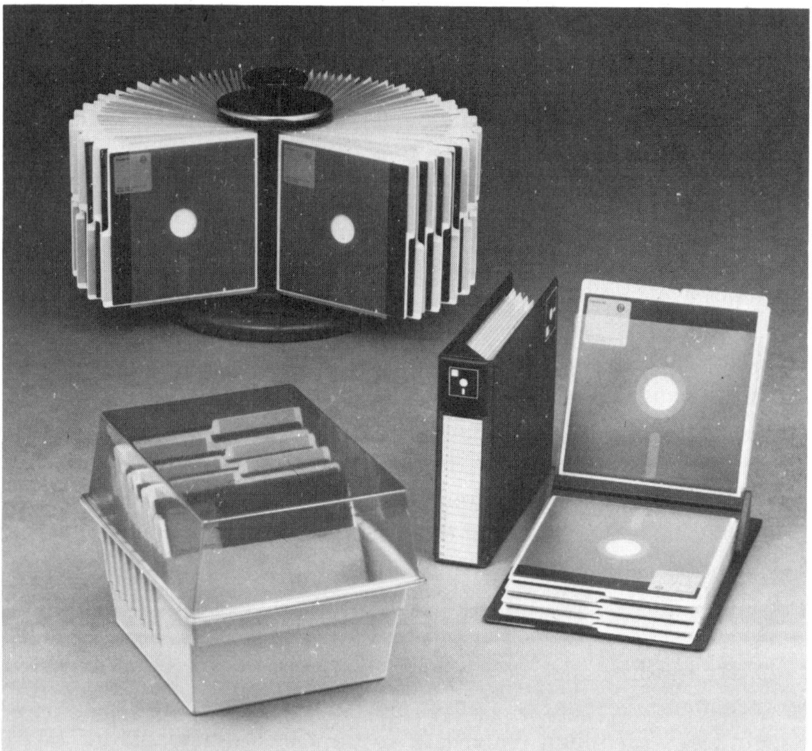

Figure 9-1 Quite a variety of floppy-disk management schemes are on the market to address your needs and budget. Consider future requirements carefully before committing to one approach. (Courtesy of Ring King Visibles, Inc.)

glorified versions of the packages they come in (some, in fact, can be purchased in these very containers). Generally called "library cases," these provide good protection against the elements and are probably the most cost-effective travel and shipping containers. For day-to-day use, however, they are a bit awkward; each box holds only ten diskettes. Their best use is probably archival storage and protecting your collection of sacred masters and backups.

A fancier incarnation of this concept may be found in one of Inmac's offerings, known as the "Floppy Manager" (not to be confused with a spineless administrator). It is also based on plastic boxes that hold ten diskettes, but the clever part is the fact that the units interlock both horizontally and vertically. This permits the creation of a well-organized disk library from which chunks can be taken at will for off-site storage or travel.

A number of floppy disk storage systems exist that are based on the use of individual pages or sleeves, each of which holds one or two disks. Most commonly, these take the form of three-hole-punched vinyl envelopes that accommodate an 8-inch disk (or a pair of 5-inchers) and allow them to be filed or stored in binders. These are often used for distribution diskettes, which appear inside the accompanying documentation binder.

Individual transparent envelopes can be had in a number of configurations, ranging from the type described above to those that accurately mimic Pendaflex hanging file folders. Others are designed to integrate with rotary or "lazy Susan" desk stands. Still others, very expensive by comparison, include a mu-metal lining to protect their precious contents against magnetic or static fields.

If you don't like library cases or systems involving individual plastic sleeves, there is always the traditional and inexpensive approach of simply putting them all in a box (preferably with a hinged dust cover). The disks stay in their original paper envelopes, and are simply treated as file folders. Versions of these exist from the junky to the elegant, priced accordingly. It's even possible to buy computer furniture with built-in disk-filing drawers, or little rolling stands that hold a couple of disk boxes and enable about 180 floppies to be shuttled about the room as desired.

Speaking of furniture, you can, if sufficiently paranoid and/or rich, purchase a dedicated diskette-storage cabinet with a built-in positive pressure air-circulation system that includes HEPA-standard filtering. These aren't cheap, but they will give about 400 diskettes reasonable protection against particulate contamination. And if you *really* want to protect your disks, you can buy a special-purpose fireproof media safe in putty, black, or computer blue to keep your data relatively cool while everything else is consumed in flames.

9.1.2 Mailers and Carrying Cases

Of course, diskettes don't always stay in the computer room, and there are numerous products that have been designed to protect them as they are shuttled about. There are magnetic shielded carrying cases, stylish foam-lined attaché cases with cutouts for diskette boxes, cardboard and plastic disk mailers, and plastic carrying cases designed to fit under an airplane seat. It becomes clear that the medium itself is one of the cheapest parts of the data storage problem.

9.1.3 Miscellaneous Media Accessories

Various other media-related items are available to make your operation more reliable, easier, or flashier. Here are some of the preeminent ones.

A disk head cleaning kit is a good idea. Consisting of special scrubbing disks and a bottle of cleaning solution, these kits enable a 30-second disk drive maintenance procedure that can eliminate many frustrating intermittent problems. In normal operation, heads pick up a coating of oxide from the disks, gradually moving them further and further away from the recording surface. The scrubbing action of the cleaning kit eliminates this, something that becomes dramatically evident on viewing the effect of a few cleanings on what starts out as a white pad. The cost of all this amortizes out to about a dollar per cleaning, cheap insurance by anybody's standards.

Another useful adjunct to life with floppies is a kit that permits you to do in your computer room what diskette manufacturers should routinely do in the plant: install hub reinforcing rings. These little white rings, averaging about 25 cents apiece, strengthen the Mylar media against the onslaught of poorly designed drive hubs, careless insertion, and normal wear and tear. One pair of mini-drives I owned for awhile (made by the same manufacturer that foisted these chronically retrying 8-inchers on me) had such critical hubs that the doors had to be slowly closed with an expert, gentle touch to avoid crimping the diskette. One "normal" disk insertion would ripple the whole disk surface, resulting in irrevocable "track 0" errors. The only solution, pending the elimination of the drives, was the installation of the hub reinforcing rings, a simple process involving a small applicator and a couple of minutes. But even in less abusive surroundings, they are recommended for the extension of media life. (Some top-of-the-line diskettes are now available with reinforcing rings as a standard feature.)

Much of the effort associated with magnetic media involves the attempt to keep them away from pernicious influences. You can buy little adhesive labels that remind people to keep magnetic fields away (not to mention color-coded labels for purely organizational purposes). There is probably no limit to this trend, except the long-overdue obsolescence of computer system components that incorporate moving parts and sensitive media.

9.2 PRINTER SUPPLIES AND ACCESSORIES

Another part of the system that is destined to keep you busy buying supplies is the printer. If nothing else, you have to keep feeding it paper and ribbons, and then there are extra printwheels, cleaning supplies, binders for the paper, sound and dust covers, shredders, and so on. Let's take a look at the possibilities.

9.2.1 Paper and Forms

Once upon a time, there was little to choose from when you wanted computer paper. Two sizes, two colors, a small handful of manufacturers. Now you can get it in green, orange, or black rulings, as well as blank. It can be had in a variety of weights, one to six parts, carbon or carbonless, with ragged or clean edges, and separable or inseparable ears. And there are more sizes than most users would know what to do with:

$8\frac{1}{2} \times 11$
$9\frac{1}{2} \times 11$
$9\frac{1}{2} \times 14$
$\frac{7}{8} \times 11$
$11\frac{3}{4} \times 8\frac{1}{2}$
$12 \times 8\frac{1}{2}$
$14\frac{7}{8} \times 8\frac{1}{2}$
$14\frac{7}{8} \times 11$

as well as a variety of roll sizes for users of thermal printers, teleprinters, calculators, and so on. It is no longer possible to say "I want some paper" and be understood.

For word-processing purposes, one of the favored choices is the $9\frac{1}{2}$-by 11-inch unruled, 20-pound paper with perforated ears. Since the ears are a half-inch wide, you end up with a standard paper size (a legal-size version is available as well) once they are removed. But for data-processing purposes, it makes more sense to use a lighter-weight stock (more sheets per box) that is, depending on your needs, printed with a "green bar" pattern to help the human eye follow lines across what is often a very wide page densely packed with numbers. Before selecting the paper styles you need, it is a good idea to ask your local paper vendor to bring around some samples.

A relatively recent introduction into the computer-paper market (and one that is very welcome) is the "pinfeed letterhead." Available in two forms, this allows the computer to print on good-quality bond paper under a standard printed letterhead, eliminating the need to fake it with printer fonts or individually fed single sheets of paper. One form of this, usually called *tipping,* involves the fastening of the letterheads (or envelopes, for that matter) to a low-grade carrier form that simply feeds it through the printer. An adhesive strip makes the connection and in a good-quality product leaves no residue. The advantage of this approach is the ability to use virtually any grade of paper, including your existing stock stationery. The disadvantage is the relative awkwardness of it and the difficulty that some printers (cheap ones, in particular) have in handling it properly.

The second technique is simply a variation on the normal continuous form that happens to leave very smooth edges after separation of pages and ears. This is generally available only in a limited range of styles, grades, and colors, but is considerably cheaper and presents no special handling problems. There are trade-offs everywhere.

Just about anything can be made into a continuous form these days, and this includes, in addition to all the standard business forms, Rolodex and index cards, self-mailers, postcards, gummed labels in dozens of styles and sizes (even tape reel labels), envelopes, and more. One particularly clever form appears in the Fidelity catalog of data- and word-processing products—a "universal form" that can become just about anything, depending on how you print it.

9.2.2 Binders

Printout binders may be had in a dizzying variety of styles, with cover materials of "genuine pressboard," flexible or rigid plastic, vinyl-coated cardboard, aluminum, and probably somewhere, wood. These are a necessity and can be found in all the common paper sizes in styles that either stand alone or fit into integrated filing systems (see Section 9.3.2).

9.2.3 Ribbons, Printwheels, and Accessories

The more robust supply catalogs will be found to contain two to four pages of printer ribbon cross-reference guide. This is quite useful but occasionally frustrating: I recently acquired a small, late-model printer for a portable word-processing application. It's quite a nice little machine for this particular point in the evolution of the technology, but the ribbons! They are identical philosophically to those that my rugged old Diablo used, and for which I paid an average of $4 to $5 apiece. But these are *fifteen bucks!* Every time a new catalog comes, I scan the listings in vain, hoping for an alternative to the "full-retail" computer store in the fancy suburban shopping center nearby. No luck. (If you want to marvel at clever design sometime, by the way, carefully pry open a continuous fabric ribbon cassette. Expecting a couple of neat little reels?)

Some money can be saved by making use of re-inked ribbons (save your empties, by all means, even if *you* don't want to re-use them). It is difficult to find re-inked ribbons of comparable quality to new ones, except in the film or "multi-strike" style, where the ribbon itself is replaced. But in heavy use, especially for internal documents, they can represent a considerable cost-reduction step.

Incidentally, if you do keep a stock of ribbons around the office, try to control the inventory in a FIFO fashion. Ink will eventually dry out, and ribbons sitting on the shelf for years will become less and less useful.

The other "plug-in" accessories for printers are, in the case of daisy-wheel and golfball types, replacement character sets. Daisy wheels in particular have grown in prominence over the years, offering a reasonably satisfying trade-off of speed and print quality pending the development of low-cost, high-density dot-matrix equipment. As such, it is possible to buy replacement printwheels in the $5 to $75 range, with dozens of type styles to choose from. The high-priced end of the spectrum corresponds to rugged metal printwheels which, considering the remarkable reliability of the plastic types, are of questionable cost-effectiveness (and they are generally not directly interchangeable anyway, something to note when purchasing a printer). Naturally, you can augment your purchase of space wheels, NEC-style "thimbles," or Selectric ball elements with the acquisition of appropriately styled binders to keep them in.

The only remaining items in this category are the various products designed to allow you to clean your typefaces. There seem to be two basic ways to do this: use swabs moistened with solvent, or run a special "paper" through the machine and print on it without a ribbon. Unless you are using a line printer, you are not likely to experience a particularly *strong* need for these products.

9.2.4 Auxiliary Equipment

There are a host of accessories for paper handling and improving the efficiency of your printer. Let's look at a few. Printers tend to make a racket, something that can become particularly annoying if they are in an office rather than a room of their own. To help with this problem, a number of manufacturers have created acoustically shielded printer enclosures designed to fit some of the more popular printers. They claim 70 to 80 percent noise reduction, and can very effectively reduce the sound pollution, changing the sound of a daisy-wheel unit, for example, from a clatter to a whisper. They're not cheap, but neither are the nerves of your personnel.

So much for the top side of the printer. Now, what's under it? For a variety of reasons, printers don't do terribly well on tables and desks: there needs to be a convenient paper path; the support should be rigid; it helps to have easy all-around access, and so on. Accordingly, there are numerous printer stands available that not only provide a strong free-standing support, but also allow the addition of a paper basket. Many units are designed to be stylistically consistent with a family of computer room furniture as well. If you want to go all the way, you can also buy a custom-tailored printer mat to go between the printer and the stand, reducing vibration and preventing creeping.

Paper baskets can be acquired even if you don't want an accompanying stand, with various designs available to hang on the back of a table, rest on the floor, or rest on a cart. Some include an inverted-vee-shaped bottom to encourage proper paper refolding.

Speaking of carts, there are even little wagons on the market that are designed to allow easy movement of paper boxes (or *very* large listings).

Once the paper has made it through the printer, there are a number of things you can do with it before throwing it in someone's IN basket. First, there is the decollator (or deleaver), which permits multipart forms to be converted into stacks of single-part forms. Versions exist that accommodate carbon or carbonless forms, and you can buy an effective hand-crank version for about half the price of a motorized unit. This is one of those tasks that is a pain without the proper equipment, but it can be done: if you have infrequent decollating requirements and are working with a two-part carbon form, there's a trick. Drive a nail into the end of a 12- to 16-inch piece of 1-inch dowel (a broomstick works fine), chuck it into a variable-speed electric drill, start the paper in three stacks (output 1, input, and output 2), and tape the end of the carbon paper to the dowel. All you have to do is keep the dowel turning at a comfortable rate and swing it gently back and forth to separate the forms into two neat stacks. It's anything but elegant, but it is most definitely cost-effective.

Another common requirement is a forms "burster," which for a thousand dollars or so will enable you to take those freshly decollated stacks of fanfold paper and convert them into stacks of individual sheets without all those annoying ears. This provides an aesthetically pleasing alternative to tearing everything apart by hand, especially if you are trying to minimize the obviousness of computer use (although why someone would want to do that, I'm not sure).

Finally, there is the venerable "un-printer," otherwise known as the shredder. When your printed information has outlived its usefulness (or when your shipping department is out of packing material), you can feed listings into these units and be rewarded with giant bags of $\frac{1}{4}$-inch strips of paper. This is the end of the line, the restorer of randomness, the agent of entropy. Nobody should be without one.

9.3 COMPUTER ROOM FURNITURE

Somewhere back in Chapter 2, we spoke of computer room layout and the need for efficiency; then in Chapter 5 we rhapsodized for a while about ergonomics and human comfort. This is where much of that meets the bottom line: the acquisition of computer room furniture.

9.3.1 Workstations and Desks

A lot has happened in the computer furniture business since the old days of plopping terminals down on desks. There is still that option, of course, but for extended operating comfort and efficiency, some of the differences between traditional office furniture and that which is appropriate for the computer age must be recognized.

Some of the problems introduced by extended CRT use are associated with the fact that the operator tends to remain in the same position much longer than was the case BC (before computers). This leads to back strain, leg cramps, a sore neck, numb buttocks, cobwebs, and attitude problems. In addition, the terminal screen can cause all forms of eyestrain, some of which are simply due to reflection and glare.

As such, there has been a rush to supply the market with flexible and comfortable workstations, and it is eminently worthwhile to consider them if you are planning on closeting someone in the computer room full time. The top-of-the-line units include not only a terminal desk, but places for disks, a printer stand, filing space, manual and listing racks, a tilt/turntable for the CRT, cable clips, power outlet strips, and an adjustable swivel chair.

Units like that are designed to accommodate an entire system and may not be appropriate for a simple data-entry station. For these applications, there are CRT-only units, such as the one pictured here from Uarco (Figure

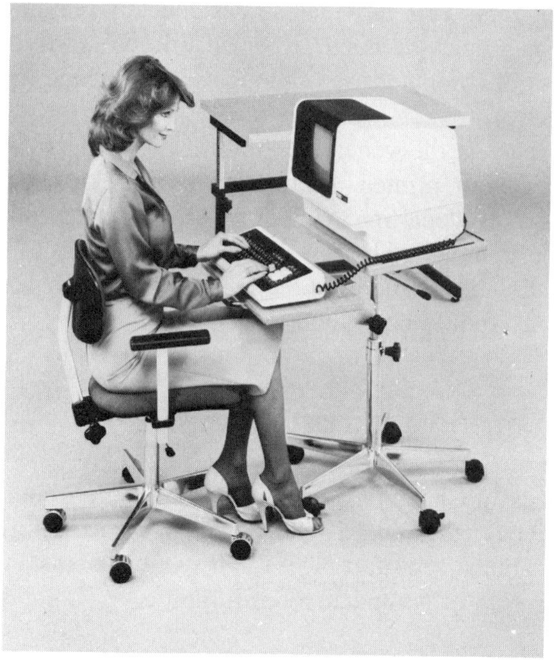

Figure 9-2 The ergonomic workstation permits easy adjustment of all critical operating dimensions (see Figure 5-1). (Courtesy of Uarco, Incorporated, 121 North Ninth Street, Dekalb, IL 60115.)

9-2). This unit permits virtually complete adjustment of the "interface" between the operator and the terminal, which, if properly used, can significantly extend the number of hours someone can survive before collapsing in agony.

There are a lot of accessories that can similarly contribute to comfortable computer use, with or without fancy workstations. The CRT turntable is one, although there are more and more terminals appearing on the market with separate keyboards and tiltable screens. There is a CRT visor available for glare reduction, as well as polarizing screens that can be fastened over the existing faceplate (Figure 9-3). There are desk organizers of all descriptions, copyholders (some of which are even electric, with a motorized reference bar controlled by a foot pedal), wrist rests to minimize wrist strain, footrests to minimize leg strain, and trays that mount on top of the terminal, presumably to give the operator a place for completed work. (Watch out with these; blocking the terminal's ventilation slots can be disastrous.)

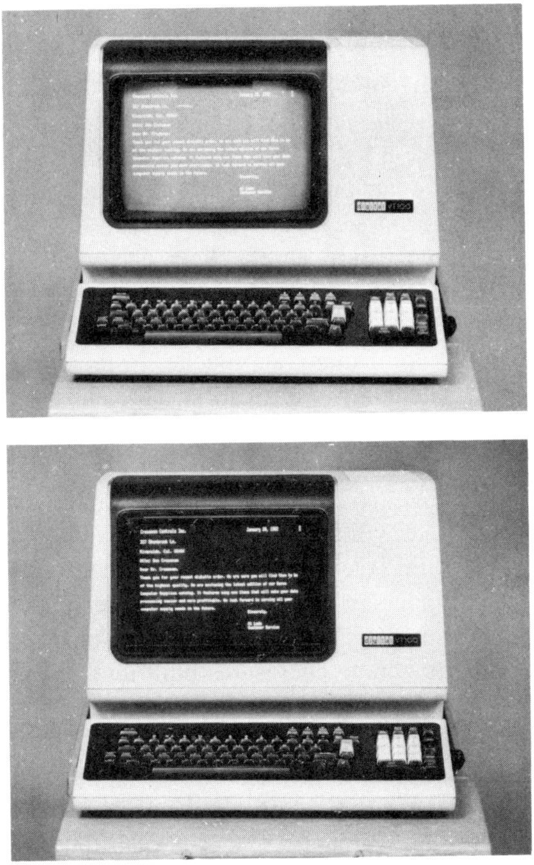

Figure 9-3 An easy solution to screen glare problems may be had in the form of polarizing filters that can be directly attached to the CRT faceplate. (Photo courtesy of Uarco, Incorporated, 121 North Ninth Street, Dekalb, IL 60115.)

9.3.2 Filing Cabinets and Racks

Back in Section 9.2.2, we dedicated a paragraph to binders, essentially passing the buck to this section. There are a lot of ways to handle the problem of proliferating paper, some of them even efficient. Forget file folders, stacks, and three-hole punching; there are enough methods around that cater specifically to computer paper that such partial solutions are no longer necessary. At the very least, invest in a stock of pressboard binders to keep printouts organized.

The main problem arises when the number of these binders begins to get out of hand. This can easily happen in even a very small business: three or four years' worth of inventory records, customer files, statements, payroll records, spread sheets, and sales data can amount to a rather impressive pile of paper. Similarly, a software-development or word-processing environment will produce reams of output that can't be thrown away.

The solution is a printout binder filing system that is easy to use and expandable. Wright-Line makes an excellent one, replete with integrated office furniture (free-standing printout racks, small units for desks, etc.), and there is another widely marketed unit based on something called a "T-Bar." These are only two of many approaches to the same basic problem, providing a means of hanging binders in an efficient fashion that doesn't interfere with their normal use.

Once a system has been chosen, you can typically find all sorts of accessories. In the case of the T-Bar units, for example, you can buy a unit called a "data center" that will hold 37,000 pages, add-on modules for that (12,000 pages each), rolling racks that hold 3600 sheets, a tabletop reference system that holds six binders, a small tabletop unit reminiscent of Pendaflex files, cabinets in a variety of sizes (in putty, sage, or black, with optional teakwood top), printout storage enclosures built into desks, and so on. It's all very well thought out, and is based on a relatively simple mechanism that allows binders to be dropped into parallel rails in a hanging file fashion or slipped horizontally into mating tracks.

Naturally, you can get as hard-core as you like with this sort of thing, including locked, fireproof cabinets. The important thing is settling on one system and sticking with it.

9.4 MISCELLANEOUS COMPUTER ROOM ACCESSORIES

And now, after all the other categorizable items, we come to that vast category called "miscellaneous." It's a full one. With no avowed organizational scheme, let's look at some of the gadgets and accessories that can make your operation more cost-effective, easier, quieter, faster, cheaper, or more stylish.

In our chapter of horror stories (Chapter 2), we spent quite a bit of time discussing static and other unpleasant effects. There are some things you can do about it.

Cheapest, and not dramatically effective, is antistatic spray (Figure 9-4). The idea here is the addition of a conductive coating to your entire environment, giving static a place to go before you reach out to touch a diskette or the system cabinet.

Figure 9-4 Antistatic spray is a temporary but inexpensive cure for the problems associated with low humidity and carpeting. (Photo courtesy of Uarco, Incorporated, 121 North Ninth Street, Dekalb, IL 60115.)

The next level is the addition of an antistatic mat to the workstation area. These can be had in a variety of styles and costs, including a clear vinyl type that is visually equivalent to the traditional chair mat.

Finally, you can cover the floor of the computer room with antistatic carpeting, either by buying antistatic throw rugs or by going for broke and doing it wall to wall.

While protecting the system against evil electrical influences, you might also look at some of the surge protectors that are available. Nothing fancy here; they generally consist of a box or similar enclosure with a plug and one or more sockets, and some circuitry inside that consumes noise spikes before they can make their way inside your system. Cheap insurance. Fancy versions can be had that also include noise filtering, ground-fault detection, and other power-related problems.

If you are concerned about the quality of your power, there are a few diagnostic tools that can be put to use. If you have a lot of money, you can buy a Dranetz Universal Disturbance Analyzer (Figure 9-5) to tell you a lot more about the power than the electric company itself knows. For about

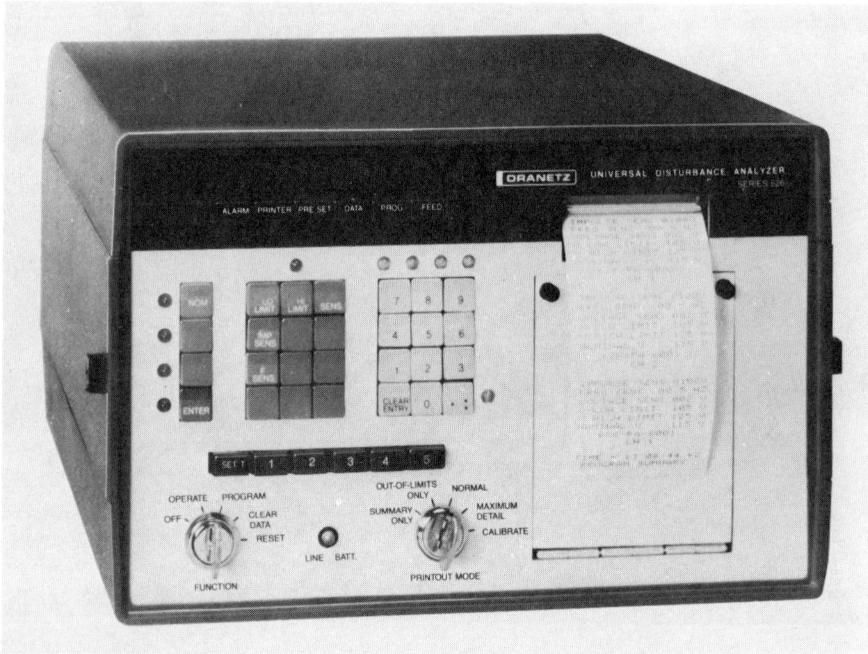

Figure 9-5 Serious power-line problems can be diagnosed with the aid of a universal disturbance analyzer, such as this unit from Dranetz. (Courtesy of Dranetz Engineering Laboratories, Incorporated.)

10% of that cost, you can pick up a little unit from Inmac (Figure 9-6) that has six lights to indicate a power failure, low line voltage, high line voltage, a spike, a drop, or high-frequency noise. This unit can pay for itself the first time you eliminate flaky software or hardware as the cause of reliability's problems and rewire the air conditioner instead.

Speaking of power lines, you can get them from place to place in your computer room (noisy or not) with a few useful accessories. First, a bag of adhesive-backed cable clips somewhere will be appreciated time and again. Second, on those annoying occasions when running a wire across the floor appears to be unavoidable, life will be much easier with the aid of a few feet of "cable bridge," molded rubber strips that contain one or two channels for the passage of power or data cables. Not only will this protect the wires and prevent people from tripping, but OSHA will love you. Finally, the dangerous profusion of "cube taps" can be eliminated with the use of a switched multiple outlet box. These can be had from the computer supply companies, or for about half the price from Heathkit or Radio Shack stores.

Figure 9-6 A low-cost power-line monitor will identify the major causes of power problems by "latching" on an LED when a disturbance occurs. (Courtesy of InMAC.)

Data cables are always in short supply, and it's a good idea to keep a few extras around (if you're handy with a soldering iron, all you need is some length of raw cable and a few RS-232 connectors of both sexes). One accessory I have found extremely useful is a collection of "gender changers" and jumper plugs, which enables the interconnection of terminals and modems in odd ways without having to put together a custom cable.

Other cable-related accessories include nylon cable ties and clips for dressing up the clutter behind the desk, junction boxes, wall plates, and switch boxes. This last item is very useful, and most commonly just allows a selection between two terminals, a terminal and a modem, or whatever. But with a little imagination and a soldering iron (or a comparable amount of money), you can put together a "universal" box that will handle any strange combination of serial lines you might need to concoct. Here, for example, I have almost daily occasion to switch from the normal word-processing relationship between terminal and CPU to one that lends itself well to the use of electronic mail and on-line data bases. After swapping plugs around one time too many, I put together a simple box with a few switches and RS-232 connectors, and now I no longer have to leave my chair. It's not very healthy, but it's quicker.

Back to system protection. A Halon fire extinguisher, of course, is *de rigueur,* and some kind of smoke or fire alarm is equally useful. We extolled the virtues of Halon earlier in the book; let's just underscore that with the comment that this is not a place to economize.

A good lock for the door is desirable, and the famous Code-a-Sentry unit can be purchased by mail order through the supply catalogs. Others of similar philosophy exist; just make sure that the code can be easily changed to lock out ex-employees whose motives may no longer match your own.

A vacuum cleaner is not a bad thing to have around, especially one that includes a long, skinny nozzle for insertion into printers and other tight spots. Dust, although generally not conductive and thus no *immediate* threat, is nevertheless very capable of blocking normal convective cooling action and interfering with mechanical operation. A vacuum cleaner is almost essential for its efficient removal.

You can keep some of the dust out, of course, by using antistatic vinyl dust covers. There are dozens to choose from, each custom-fitted to a particular terminal or printer. These offer the added benefit of shunning coffee spills (although in all fairness, I have to observe that there is probably not much coffee being consumed when the units are covered up).

Speaking of terminal cleanliness (sounds like the result of a strict upbringing), there are CRT screen cleaning kits available that include lint-free wipes and a special fluid. CRT faceplates do tend to pick up dust, cigarette-smoke goo, and fingerprints, and after a while these form an annoying haze between the operator and the characters.

In addition to all these items for computer protection, connection, and sanitation, there are a number of convenient accessories for computer *use,* which is what all this is supposedly about in the first place. If you're a programmer, for example, you'll get considerable mileage out of a hex/octal/binary calculator that allows the manipulation of addresses and other numbers in a fashion that matches the system notation. The TI LCD Programmer and the remarkable HP-16C exemplify this breed, with the latter offering programmability and a number of extra features that make it very useful for system design and debugging.

If you have occasion to draw flowcharts, you can find a number of different styles of templates, all of which are descendants of the venerable old IBM flowcharting template that has been around forever. If you don't like that approach, there are blueline forms available with nested flowcharting symbols gridded across the page, providing a nonreproducible guide for hand-drawn but neat layouts. Padded forms are also available to aid with CRT display design, page layout, and program coding.

An invaluable aid to forms design (and word processing) is the forms ruler, available in many different styles. Basic requirements are a 10-pitch scale for horizontal character placement and a $\frac{1}{6}$-inch scale for vertical layout, as well as standard English and metric rulings.

At some point, this would degenerate into a discussion of office supplies, so let's quit while we're ahead. Clearly, there are a number of items available that can increase the efficiency of a small-system installation, and I strongly recommend writing to the companies listed in Appendix A for their catalogs.

Epilogue

With that, we end this discussion of the "glue" necessary to hold a microsystem installation together. None of it is as exciting as that gleaming new machine on the desk, nor is it likely to be addressed in any kind of serious manner by the average computer vendor. But this book holds the keys to a successful installation: from keeping a clean machine to avoiding human conflict, these are the issues that can spell the difference between a system that *really* works and one that doesn't.

Every installation is different, of course, and I would hardly suggest that the various procedures and practices in this book are universally applicable. Instead, I have attempted to call your attention to the potential problems and then propose solutions that, in most cases, work. No guarantees . . . except perhaps that an awareness of the whole story can help you spot trouble long before it has a chance to turn into a disaster.

Good luck!

Appendix A

Computer supply catalogs may be obtained from:

Inmac
2465 Augustine Drive
Santa Clara, CA 95051

Misco
P.O. Box 399
Holmdel, NJ 07733

Moore
P.O. Box 20,
Wheeling, IL 60090

NCR
P.O. Box 550, Centerville Station
Dayton, OH 45459

Pryor
8785 North Port Washington Road,
Milwaukee, WI 53217

Uarco
121 North Ninth Street
DeKalb, IL 60115

Appendix B

THE GLITCH-GUARD

In Chapter 2, I suggested a simple power glitch protection device that effectively turns short interruptions into long ones. This is hardly a stand-alone solution to power problems, but it can eliminate many of the damaging effects of brief "dropouts." There are at least two popular CRT terminals on the market (and one matrix printer) that are virtually guaranteed to require repair after removal and immediate reapplication of power, and some disk drives have a strong propensity for writing spurious noise on the media under similar circumstances.

The circuit is simply a "latching relay" that remains energized under normal conditions. When power fails, it deenergizes and awaits manual

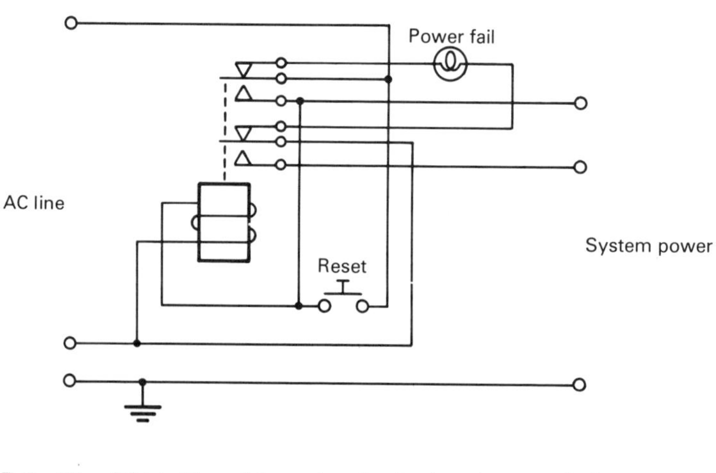

Figure B-1 The Glitch-Guard is a simple device that can help prevent system damage due to short power interruptions. It can be built for around $10.

depression of a pushbutton before power is reapplied to the load. During this "off" period, a light is illuminated to indicate the status of the unit.

The Glitch-Guard (Figure B-1) can be handily assembled in just about any enclosure, even a sufficiently large multiple-outlet box. The relay should have a 115-volt ac coil and double-pole double-throw contacts rated at about 10 amperes for the average installation.

Index

Index

Index